CW00322006

7

Senior
GOLFER

Senior
GOLFER

GUINNESS PUBLISHING

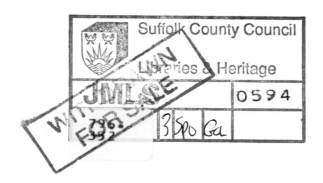
© SP Creative Design 1994

Published in Great Britain by Guinness Publishing Ltd,
33 London Road, Enfield, Middlesex

Jacket design by Pat Gibbon

Cover photograph at Enfield Golf Club. Thanks to Mr. M.J. Ormes,
Mrs. P.J. Williams, Mr. F.L. and Mrs. E.M. Montgomery, and
Secretary/Manager Nigel Challis for their participation and
co-operation. Photography by Mike Good.

Designed and produced by SP Creative Design
Linden House, 147 Kings Road
Bury St Edmunds, Suffolk, England
Editor: Heather Thomas
Art Director: Rolando Ugolini
Photography by Rolando Ugolini and Mark Shearman

A catalogue record for this book is available from the
British Library

ISBN 0-85112-731-2

Printed in Italy by New Interlitho SPA, Milan

Contents

The set up	7
The swing	25
The long game	47
The short game	73
Common faults	115
Trouble shots	131
Practice	143

The authors

Les Jones

Les Jones is the Golf Professional at Woodbridge Golf Club, Suffolk. He was Head of the Swing Department for the PGA Tutorial Body from 1989 to 1992, and had been a PGA Swing Instructor for eighteen years. He has won the Middlesex Professional Championship and has been Suffolk Open Champion on four consecutive occasions. Les has wide experience of teaching Senior players. As a Senior player himself, he has experienced may of the problems that most Seniors encounter.

Tony Moore

Tony Moore is the Head Golf Professional at St Mellion Golf Club, Cornwall, England. He coaches the county teams of both Devon and Cornwall and has taught several well-known golfers including Roger Winchester and Jonathan Langlead, the English Amateur Champion. Tony is a Senior player and coaches many Seniors.

The set up

By Les Jones

hen talking in the locker room to senior members of my club, I was asked my definition of a 'Senior' player.

After a short thought my answer was: "When you have played squash to a reasonable standard and the young bucks begin to run you ragged round the court, and your physical and mental recovery rate lasts through the next day.

"When you play tennis and you can no longer get to the serve or return serve and begin to feel the strain after a couple of sets.

"When you have played golf to a high standard and your handicap goes up, and you can't hit the ball as far as you used to, and the game becomes frustrating."

If you are experiencing these difficulties, then maybe you have become a senior. If you are a mature person, perhaps on the point of retiring and you are unused to regular sport or exercise you may start to think: "What shall I do now to take up a sports activity?"

If you have not played golf before, why not give it a try? It is a game that is played at a sedate pace. It gives you all the exercise you want in lovely surroundings, but much more than that, it offers you a great challenge: mastering technique, controlling the flight of the ball, judging distance, increasing your self-control, improving by practice and professional teaching. This is the direction in which you must go if you have not played before; golf is interesting, satisfying and enjoyable.

If you are an established golfer, I have one word of advice – adapt. We will cover this subject as we progress through the book.

Before you start, having the right equipment is of paramount importance. There is so much equipment available these days that you should not just buy any set of clubs that you see. If you are starting out in golf or just getting on a bit and you want to change your clubs go and have a chat with your professional. By looking at your swing, the club and some hit shots he may want to make some adjustment to your action. Then – and only then – will he advise you on the correct weight, shaft, grip and angles of loft and lie that are right for you. You can purchase a set of clubs that suit you in every way. The clubs may look very nice and may boost your confidence, but they are only wood, rubber and metal, and it is only with the performance of your swing that you will bring them to life so that they feel an integral part of your anatomy – literally, an extension of yourself.

Many books and teaching tips have been written through the years, on the importance of the correct set up, and many points have been repeated time and time again. Why? Because they are so important. I would like to run through these basics with you again, with particular reference to the senior golfer.

The set up

This requires static positions and angles in preparation to stand to the ball correctly so that you may hit it in the desired direction. For the beginner these disciplines may feel strange at first, even to the point of feeling awkward. For the established player, they need to be checked to ensure that certain positions are always maintained. This can be done at home in the garden or indoors during quiet moments. If you can find a few minutes each day to practise your set up and follow a set pattern, you will find that there will be less fiddling and thinking about it when you set up on the tee. 'Feel' will take over and you will go through the motions automatically so that at the moment of truth when you are setting yourself up to hit the ball you will be more relaxed. Relaxation is vital as it plays a very large part in allowing freedom of movement and co-ordination when swinging the club.

Above: This senior golfer has quite a good set up. His arms are a little stiff and his knees have not flexed as much as we would like, but he is on target. The head position is good with the chin off the chest, and the spinal angle is good apart from the flexation of the knees. He is standing the correct distance from the ball.

Static positions and angles

Let us run through the set-up positions now. There is a lot to think about but very soon you will feel more comfortable about them as all the parts fit into a correct sequence and complement each other.

1. Aim

Aim the club head(blade) with a 7 or 8 iron; the bottom leading edge should be at right angles to the target. To get used to this, select several objects in different directions and line up the blade behind a tee peg or ball, and then the bottom leading edge to the target. You then have the imaginary ball-to-target line that is used for each shot you play with irons.

Right: The position of the blade is square to the ball-to-target line. The left-hand grip is very good whereas the right-hand grip is erring a little bit on the strong side. The stance and alignment are good with the feet and shoulders parallel. Note the head position with the chin off the chest creating a relaxed feeling. The shoulder angle is correct with the right shoulder slightly lower than the left. The left arm is comfortably straight, the right arm comfortably bent. The 'V' created between the wrists and shoulders is ideal. The feet, knees, hips and shoulders are all parallel to the ball-to-target line – a good set up.

2. The hold

The hold (grip) on the club needs to be correct as it is this that controls the face of the club head. However good your swing is, a bad hold can badly affect the control and flight of the ball. Study the hold, take a positive view of what you need to do and don't fiddle about.

Left hand

In practising the hold, take the club in your left hand (right-handed player), two inches down the shaft, with the back of the left hand facing the target. The thumb will rest on the grip right of centre. By looking straight down at your hand you will see two knuckles of the hand showing, and the 'V'

created between the thumb and forefinger will point between the chin and the right shoulder. Look at the photographs and use them as a visual aid to achieve this position. The correct positioning of the left thumb is essential as you need to marry the right hand to this.

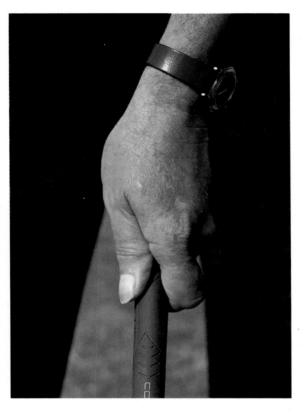

Above: Two knuckles are clearly visible, and the left hand is parallel to the ball-to-target line. The thumb is slightly down the right-hand side of the shaft creating a 'V' between forefinger and thumb which should point between the right shoulder and head. This 'V' should be closed or it will create problems in the backswing.

Above: Side-on view of the left-hand hold. The shaft runs through the palm into the middle of the pad; not through the fingers.

Right hand

Look at the palm of your right hand. You will see two pads: the large muscle below the thumb and the smaller muscle on the left side of the hand. Look for the valley between the two pads(muscles). Now bring the palm of the hand onto the grip, the palm facing the target. The valley between the pads will completely cover the left thumb, the little finger will overlap the index finger of the left hand, and the fingers will close round the grip, with the right forefinger slightly triggered, and the right thumb to the left side of the shaft.

Finally, check that both 'V's are pointing between the chin and right

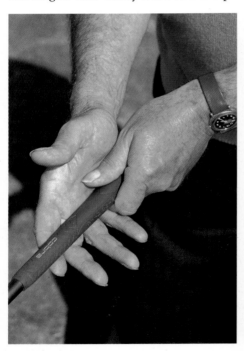

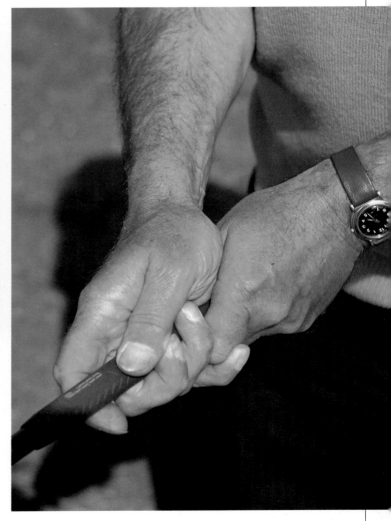

Above: With the left hand in place, position the palm of the right hand facing the target. Place the thumb between the two pads of the right hand. When the fingers are wrapped round the shaft of the club, it will be more of a finger grip than a palm grip.

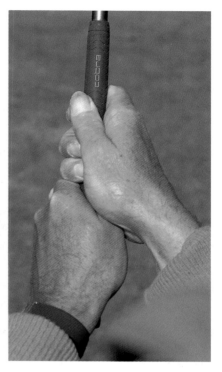

Left: Two knuckles of the left hand are visible with the back of the left hand pointing towards the target and parallel to the palm of the right hand. The thumb is completely covered and the hold is moulded for both hands to work as one. Above: The grip is good but note that the right wrist has bowed outwards, possibly because in building the hold, the arm was not correctly positioned. This will inevitably affect the backswing adversely.

Left: The right little finger is overlapping the bottom finger of the left hand. The fingers have wrapped round the shaft which is more in the fingers than the palm. The thumb of the right hand has come over to the left-hand side of the shaft, and the thumb of the left hand is covered. This position moulds both hands together to create a controlled flexible hold without any tension.

shoulder. Hold the club just for control, not grip, as if you are delivering a physical blow.

So you now have the direction in which you are going to hit the ball and the hold that is going to control the blade in the correct angle to strike the ball. Well done – next, we need to look at stance and alignment.

Above: The Vardon, or overlapping, grip. Note that the little finger of the right hand overlaps the bottom finger of the left. This is by far the most popular hold used by members of the golfing fraternity.

Above: Note the position of the head, shoulders and the 'V' created by the arms. The left arm is straight and the right one slightly bent with the elbow pointing towards the right hip. This is a very important part of the set up.

The interlocking grip

Above: The interlocking grip. The little finger of the right hand interlocks into the cleft between the first and second fingers of the left hand, instead of overlapping the bottom finger as in the Vardon grip. This hold is used by Seniors with small or weak hands and by women golfers who tend to lack the strength and power of men.

Above: This photograph clearly shows the complete formation of the fingers in the interlocking hold. You can see that it helps to mould the hands together so that they work in unison and thereby create a more effective swing.

The baseball (two-handed) grip

The baseball grip is yet another variation on the golf hold, this time with all the fingers postioned down the club shaft. This grip is occasionally recommended by some golf professionals with the purpose of creating strength and power. However, it can be a temperamental position because instead of both hands working in unison, it can easily develop into a movement where one hand works against the other. Its only hope for Seniors is in promoting more flexibility. Personally, I would never recommend it.

The left-handed grip

The left-handed grip is basically the mirror image of the right-handed hold. It is built in exactly the same way but reversing the positions. Notice that two knuckles are visible on the right hand, and the right thumb has been covered completely between the pads of the left hand. The left hand in the photograph is erring towards a strong position but this is a well-built grip.

3. Stance and alignment

The third static position now required is the stance and alignment of the body. Do you remember our imaginary 'ball-to-target' line? You may now proceed by marrying the body alignment to the ball-to-target line in the following sequence: Place your feet six to eight inches apart – your heels, knees, hips and shoulders will be parallel to the 'ball-to-target' line. An excellent way to practice this discipline is to hold the club across your shoulders so that the shaft is seen to be in this parallel position. Then lower your arms so that the line across the hips is parallel, then the knees and then the feet.

This sequence shows how to make everything parallel. Place two clubs on the ground representing the ball-to-target and stance lines. Hold the club at waist height over the ball-to-target line; lower it parallel to the stance line; raise to the shoulders and out.

4. Ball position

The ball position will be in the centre of your feet at this time. However, as you progress with longer clubs and swings, the ball position will change in relation to the feet, but we will come to that later.

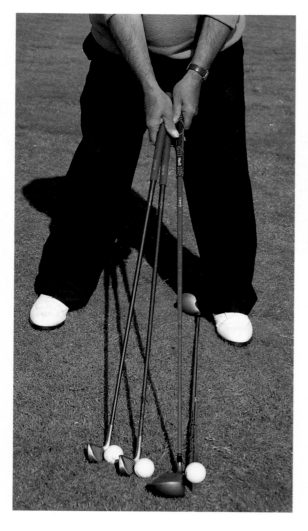

Left: The ball position will change according to length and which club you use. These are the positions for: the driver with the ball teed up inside the left heel; the medium-long iron with the ball approximately two inches behind the driver position; and the pitching clubs in the centre of the stance. The only time you work to the back of the centre is when you are manufacturing a shot. Otherwise you merely de-loft the club. At all times, with every club the position of the hands in relation to the legs remains constant, i.e. the left hand opposite the inside left leg. Above: The down-the-line angle shows how the body stays the same. The shorter the club, the nearer the ball. This changes the angle of the takeback and the line of attack.

5. Posture

Posture is the position that your body takes to complete the set up, a position that sets the pattern of your swing, and that many average players do not achieve. Many of the faults that occur in people's swings are caused by incorrect posture. To develop the correct and natural posture: take up the previous four positions as described, and then stand up straight with the club held away from you at shoulder height. Co-ordinate a bend from your waist with the arms moving down until the club head touches the ground. You then 'soften' the knees to eliminate any tension. We use the word 'soften', rather than bend or flex, because it is easier for this position to be achieved without being overdone.

Below: To find your distance from the ball, extend your arms at shoulder height. Bending from the waist, lower the club head until it touches the ground. Keep the arms married with the waist movement. Bend from the waist, not the hips.

Above: The club head is being lowered towards the ground. You can see clearly that the spinal angle is now bending towards the required position.

Above right: The club head has now touched the ground and this is the correct distance to stand from the ball. It appears at this stage that the arms are still a long way away from the ball.

Right: However, when you 'soften' your knees (do not bend them), the spinal angle and position of the lower body is complete and the correct distance from the ball is achieved in a natural comfortable position.

Now starting at the feet, you can build in other points to finish the set up. Your body weight will be evenly distributed between the feet and towards the balls of your feet; and the butt of the left hand will be opposite the inside of the left leg, approximately four to five inches away from the leg. The left arm will be hanging down in a comfortable straight position, the right arm slightly bent with the forearms close together, again in a relaxed comfortable way which feels natural, not forced. Your head will be held with the chin off the chest. Try to glance down at the ball rather than put your head down – this will allow you to swing the club back more freely.

Left and above: The set up and posture for a woman are basically the same as for a man. However, you can see here that the right arm is very stiff and straight and this could cause problems when she swings the club. This is a common fault among many Senior players who often lack suppleness. The slight flexation of the knees is not quite enough but the alignment is good as are the ball position and hold.

Building up a routine

It is important to build a pre-shot routine that works for you. The swing will follow on as part of that routine. Here the ball is being lined up to the target using a popular technique: standing behind the ball and visualizing the direction in which to aim.

Above right: Decide on direction and aim the blade towards the target. Check your hold. The sequence is initiated by the blade and the hold being in the correct positions. Right: You can now adjust the ball position in relation to your stance. Use this routine for every shot you play so that it comes naturally and automatically without even having to think about what you're doing.

Left: Open your stance and find your balance with your feet shoulder-width apart. You are now ready for action and correctly positioned for the swing.
Below: This side-on view shows that the angle between the arms and the club shaft is in the correct position. This set up lends itself to swinging the club freely into a good swing path and plane.

Summary

There seems an awful lot to do and think about, but you will find that if you practise these positions in sequence, by the time you have reached this point it will all fall into place and you will set up automatically without consciously having to think about it. You will feel relaxed and ready for action, and one of the secrets of successful golf is to stay relaxed.

By studying and practising these static exercises, you will master them and despite any difference in physique, you will look approximately the same as your fellow golfers, whatever age you may be. However, as you move into your swing, things will change and you will become yourself. You are an individual, and your swing will develop from your own physical build, strength, flexibility and natural movements. A lot of problems arise when people try to copy what other golfers do, even though it may not be viable. Please be yourself and bring out your own flair and talent, and build on these accordingly. We can't all swing like Nick Faldo and the other golfing greats – we are all built differently.

We all love to watch the great tournament players, the golfing gladiators – fit, supple, their mental and physical approach honed to perfection. They hit the ball long distances, yet that delicate touch on and around the greens is still apparent. The next time you watch them play, look again. With the exception of a small minority, they do look quite alike as they stand to the ball, but when they swing the club they vary enormously in movement and style. What are they? They are individuals who, through practice, have found the way that they can hit the ball at their best. You must do the same: find your own swing, recognise it and stay with it, as we will discover in the next chapter.

The swing

By Les Jones

Now that you feel happy with the set up, you can initiate the start of the swing. This is the area where many senior golfers experience problems or a loss of form as they grow older, often as a result of reduced strength or suppleness in the body. We will start by going through the basic technique of the swing. This is not only essential for newcomers to the game, but also for more experienced players to brush up on the basics and check that they are swinging correctly.

The waggle

This is the start of the swing. It is simply backward and forward movement with the club head, via the hands, away from the ball and back to the ball – just a short movement of a foot or so. The waggle gives you the feeling that you are in complete control of the club. It also relaxes your muscles so that you can complete the swing with smoothness and rhythm. It is difficult to achieve this from a static start, but when you waggle two or three times the muscles will tell you that it is time to go.

Right: Here the waggle is introduced with a driver. Note how far the club head has been taken back, not over-long. The head, shoulders and body remain as at address; there is no movement at all, only in the hands and a slight relaxing movement of the knees. This gives you the feel of swinging with control.
Opposite: Look at the target as you waggle. Keep your body square as at address. When you move your head to look at the target look sideways down the line; don't turn your body as well as your head as many Seniors do. From this position it is difficult to pinpoint the target although it will give you a panoramic view of the whole golf course! This fault is caused by stiff neck muscles.

The one-piece takeaway

So away we go with the left shoulder beginning to turn, the arms, hands and club head all moving together. This is called the one-piece takeaway. Take this movement to just below waist height, and you will find that other little muscles are joining in. The shoulder turn will turn the left hip slightly, the left hip will bring the left knee inwards towards the back of the ball, and the left foot will move to the inside ball of the foot. The weight will have moved to the right side, and the right hip will have moved slightly backwards. All of these later movements will be sympathetic – they will happen. Let them happen, do not give any conscious thought to them – the initial takeaway has taken care of them. The only thought you may need to look to is that the right knee will have remained flexed as it was at set up. From this short swing you will now make a short swing into and through the ball to a finish, the length of the throughswing being equal to that of the backswing.

Right: The one-piece takeaway showing the address position. This is the moment when the waggle has been completed and you are ready to go. The sequence of movements that follows is pictured opposite.
Opposite: Everything should move naturally and the movements of major muscles should move the smaller ones. The shoulders, arms, hands and club head move as one unit. Because you're moving the left shoulder this, in turn, moves the left hip slightly, which moves the left knee slightly inwards towards the ball. In turn, this moves the left foot slightly inwards and this causes the right hip to move slightly backwards, creating an automatic weight transference.

Above: This is the final position where all the movements have been achieved. It is just a continuation of the shoulder turn to the movement at the top of the swing. Note that the shoulders and arms are the dominant factors; all the other movements are sympathetic to these.

The downswing

This will be initiated by the left hip moving slightly towards the target, and bringing the weight back to the left side, which, in its turn, will bring the arms and club head into the strike zone in a gradual accelerating movement through the ball. This momentum will take you to just below waist height by which time the hips will have rotated so that your body is facing the target. Your arms will be comfortably straight, the

Above: The downswing has been initiated by a slight lateral movement of the left hip towards the target. The weight that moved into the backswing has been returned by the hip movement which has also started the arms downwards in their sweep.

Above: The club is carried on through to a position waist high, and the movements you can see must follow naturally from each other and must not be contrived.

right knee will have moved in towards the left knee. If you hold this position you will see that the blade of the club, your grip, shoulders and hips will look the same as in your set-up position.

Backswing practice

Practise this short swing as much as you can: swing backwards and forwards again, feeling the rhythm and the tempo. The club head should brush the turf as you swing through the ball position. When you can do this, then hit as many balls as you wish.

The full swing

From here, the longer swing up to the full swing is not so difficult. Just continue the shoulder turn – you will feel the cocking of the wrists, which is a gradual and natural movement (I will go into wrist action later in more depth). The arms will move upwards so that at the top of the swing your shoulders will have turned and you are looking at the ball over the left shoulder. Your arms will be in the same position as in the set up, the left arm comfortably straight, and the right arm having moved from a slightly bent to a right-angled position with the elbow pointing down towards the back of the right heel.

Of course there are other points of which you should be aware and we will consider these later on in the chapter, but

Above: The waggle has motivated the swing and the shoulder begins to move back. All the movements are together, continuing into the one-piece takeaway at waist height. The swing then continues with a left shoulder turn and the wrist action begins to cock gradually(opposite top left). Let this happen naturally; don't force it.

provided that you are correctly positioned when you set up, you will find your own top of the backswing by natural means. If you are ever in doubt, I would strongly advise that you spend half an hour with your professional. He is there to talk you through any part of the swing that may have gone slightly awry.

Above right: The shoulders move round and the wrist action continues to cock. Stiffness in the knees here makes the left knee a little unresponsive – it should move across more. This is a common problem for Seniors. Right: The top of the backswing with a 90-degree shoulder turn and 45-degree turn of the hips.

Right: The downswing is initiated by the left hip. The arms are lowered, the wrist action still fully cocked. The weight transfers but the left knee is not doing the work it should do and the swing is under pressure.

Impact and follow through

Having arrived at the top of the swing in the correct comfortable position, remember that power has been built in to your movement. Your body should be coiled and a relaxed movement has been set up. As in the shorter swing, the left hip initiates the downswing, which, in turn, transfers weight to the left side. It also brings the arms down into the hitting area where the club is released in to and through the ball. The momentum will then take the body through and release your head from its central position – you must not try to keep the head down on the throughswing – to a high finish, with the

Left: The club is released into the ball, the left leg has recovered well and the right knee moves in towards the left one.
Above: The momentum takes you through the ball and into the left side. The head is moving now with the pull of the swing and the club head; there is no resistance. The hands have moved through together without quick flicks or wrist breaks.

Below: The right knee is almost fully through and the head is almost up, with the right arm comfortably straight maintaining the radius of the swing. The *wrists have commenced their recocking movement which helps to dispel any signs of tension. Below: The posture is straightening for the finishing movement.*

Right: The swing is now completed and finishes nice and high. The body is facing the target and balanced. Rhythm and tempo have enabled this to happen.

shoulders and hips facing the target at the end. You should feel balanced.

I could write as many words again on the set up and swing, but the less thinking that you do, the less confused your mind and muscles become. Keep your practice disciplines clear and concise, and do not jump from one thing to another. So far we have studied statics and angles, and now the time has come to find out where your weaknesses are and practise no more than two points at a time. Working on just one area of weakness is even better so that in the end you will work on your tempo, rhythm and balance.

Below: Here the swing is viewed from a slightly different angle. This shows the perfect balance that you should attempt to achieve, and which lends itself to the development of precision swinging.

Above: This shows the position at the top of the backswing. The head is still and the wrist action good but because the legs are tense they have become unresponsive, *creating the problem of the arms splaying. You can see that the arms have moved apart instead of staying together as they were in the original address position.*

Above: This is not a bad position through the ball but it is a little lethargic. The hands have closed the face of the golf club, and you can see clearly that the body weight has moved on to the toe, forwards instead of sideways. This view is taken looking down the line towards the target.

Wrist action

Earlier on in this chapter, we mentioned wrist action, and this is the most flexible part of the golf swing. An enormous number of players over-emphasise this action which can, and does, cause all kinds of problems. A good exercise for checking the amount of wrist cock is to take your hold, and then hold the club out in front of you at shoulder height. Now cock the wrists until the shaft is pointing to the sky – that is the natural full cock position. You will see that if you try to move them any more than this, the arms will begin to splay sideways and the shape of your hold will change.

Go through this routine again. When the shaft is pointing to the sky, turn your left shoulder, which will take you into the top-of-the-swing position. Your wrist action should be at right angles and in a fully cocked position. You may feel this much less than you normally do, and you should make time to practise it.

An exercise for wrist action: hold the club straight out in front and cock the wrists until the shaft points skywards. Turn the left shoulder to achieve the top of the backswing position shown here.

The arms

The arms create the radius of the swing. Your left arm is comfortably straight at address and remains constant throughout the backswing and downwards to impact and just beyond, when the right arm takes over to complete the radius on the throughswing. Together, they play the vital role of co-ordinating the wrist action to the body movement; the better the arms work, the more consistent the whole swing becomes.

Right: The left arm is hanging down comfortably from the shoulders; it is straight but not stiff. In this position the arm creates the radius of the swing. In the movement through, the right arm maintains that radius through the ball.

Problems for seniors

Starting to play golf as a senior is the same as for a younger person taking up the game. The basic fundamentals of the game and the skills are the same; the only difference is in the suppleness of the body and if you have physical problems that may impede or interfere with your general flexibility. We have already dealt with the set up and the swing. Following the disciplines in sequence you may find that you cannot move into the so-called top of the backswing, or achieve a full-blooded follow through, both of which the younger players do with such ease. No matter; you can still play this game of golf well enough to enjoy it.

Physical build

Let us look first at your physical build. You may be a short stocky person. When you set yourself up to hit the ball you should feel comfortable and relaxed but because of your build you will tend to plant yourself with the feet too wide. We talk about the feet being the width of your walk, or shoulder width, for full shots. Too wide a stance could be one of the causes of restricted swinging. To err

The stance is too wide and this makes the whole movement unresponsive. The knees cannot work and in trying to achieve a good backswing, everything is thrown out of gear. The feet are too wide and this makes it almost impossible to have any fluency of movement at all.

slightly on the narrow side would help the movement of the lower half of the body, i.e. the feet, knees, legs and hips will move much more freely. You want to feel alive at and below the waist throughout the swing.

　　If your physique is tall or you are slim, the action will be a little more loose. Keep this feeling and work on your tempo; the two points to work on are the shoulder turn to 90 degrees, but not in a forced manner, and the arms. These help to maintain the radius of the backswing. So swing it, but do not put yourself under pressure with the arms and wrists; a three-quarter position is in

the safety zone and will still give you ample power. You can then release the club head from this position into and through the ball at a far more controlled tempo than if you were fighting the swing. It is easier to move further through the ball because of the momentum, so do not try to restrict this

momentum – just let it flow and you will then find a natural finish that becomes repetitive and thereby consistent. Any attempt to move through physically will be almost certain to produce a high percentage of indifferent and bad shots. Play within yourself.

Restricted swing

If you have been a good or steady golfer throughout what we might call your earlier years, and you find that you are not hitting the ball so far with your woods, long and medium irons, and even the 9 iron you think you hit 150 yards, do not despair. Nor should you strive to be the same as you used to be. If you came to me and asked, like many senior golfers do, "Can you make me hit the ball further?", in most cases I would say "No." "Why?" you may ask. The simple answer is that the muscles throughout the body have stiffened. Maybe this has been happening over the last year or so and has not been noticed until now. Your reflexes

have become slower, which in turn means that the swing will be slower. Therefore you have lost length, not enough to be serious but enough to hurt your pride more than anything else. Now is the time to adapt; it is not all doom and gloom. In fact, the challenge becomes as exciting as ever it was. Accept that possibly you will be restricted in your swing; and that you are going to lose a few yards. You can still strike the ball more accurately than you used to when you were younger. You will not lose your touch round the greens, and if you think right, you may be a little more canny.

Opposite: The safety zone is a position at the top of the swing achieved by the shoulder turn through 90 degrees and the hips through 45 degrees. The arms and wrist action are good and there is no need to strive for a longer swing. There is adequate power in this movement for any Senior player. To strive for a longer swing to hit the ball further would be to court disaster.

Just a little story....

I am a senior, and throughout my golfing career I have hit the ball well, although sometimes a little wayward. I was long in every department. Some four years ago I developed knee trouble, and after a couple of years I had operations on them, and for a while I could not play any golf. However, things became a little better and I practised for limited periods. After falling base over apex a few times, I began to make contact with the ball. I then sat down and took a good look at myself; I knew that I must adapt and use what I have got. I am much shorter with the long clubs, about the same with the 100-yard shots, my backswing is shorter too, but I have become much more aware of my hands and arms. My knees keep me rather static on the backswing and hence the lack of length in the take back, but because of the momentum on the downswing the lower half of the body moves freely. Score wise this is coming back; I can now manage 16 holes

Below: The position of release through the ball. You will note that the knees have allowed the head and the body to remain behind the ball with an arched back.

and the card looks good – pars and birdies with perhaps a 7 or 8 on a couple of holes due to the fact that my concentration was a little lax and my muscles tried to do what they used to do, which leads to disaster!

So if you too have leg or knee troubles, try working more with the top half of the

Above: A restricted leg movement. The right knee has stayed fairly straight, restricting the rotational movement through the ball. The player is fighting to retain balance.

body – shoulders, arms and hands. If you have problems with the wrists or arms, the lower part of the body should be more active.

The mind game

Once you have sorted out any little problems in your swing and you are relaxed and happy with the way you are striking the ball, to help you to score better you must have a good mental attitude, and this is what I call

'the thinking game'. There follows several instances when shots can be saved by planning which shot you should play and which shot you should not.

You have hit the ball into the rough,

the ball is not lying too well, and you can reach the green with a 5 iron. If it comes off, great! However, the chances of success are against you. Take a 9 iron, and pick the spot that gives you the best line to the pin. Result: you have played a safe shot out of trouble, you feel good because you are in position to play on to the green, and therefore you still feel relaxed and confident. But if you have hit the 5 iron into further trouble you will become agitated. It may take two or three holes to settle down again, so don't be greedy – play it safe.

A second shot to the green, and it's a long shot; the pin is on the left side of the green guarded by bunkers. If you hit a super shot you can make the green. The club you require is a 3 wood , and it has got to be good. Danger signals are flashing, and your rhythm and tempo could be lost here. Just think about it: a steady 5 wood short right of the green puts you in with a chance, and that is all it is, of a chip and putt. Again, think how many times have you faced this shot and approached it with the thought: "I must get down in two". However, this raises that ugly word tension. Look at it this way and say to yourself: "If I can get down in two I will save a shot". We know that the object

is to get down in a chip and putt, but the word 'must' can upset the smoothness of your movement.

When playing short shots round the green so many of you try to play lofted clubs. The master players play these shots a lot, and they practise for hours to capture the degree of finesse required to reach the perfection that they achieve. What I recommend to you is that you should pitch only when you have to – the chip and run is far safer. A club like a 7 iron used with a putting stroke gives a better percentage of control, especially if you do not have sufficient practice.

When playing shots over a bunker on to the green, gather your thoughts; use the bunker as a guide to gauge your shot, not as a trap that you must get over. Again, the way you think can give you either a relaxed approach or a tense staccato shot.

To stop a ball quickly on the greens you will need a good line, a good strike and soft greens. These three points do not always come together. Look at the shot differently and ask: "How much green have I got to play with and how much room have I got to let the ball run?" It is again the easier shot for you to play.

The long game

By Tony Moore

I am sure that you will have come across the much used saying that 'you drive for show but putt for dough', the inference being that although a long drive down the centre of the fairway is very spectacular, the putting (the business end of the game) is far more important in compiling a good score.

It is very hard to argue against this because, in essence, this statement is perfectly correct. However, the two parts of the adage must go hand in hand. If you keep duffing your tee shots into the rough or slicing them out of bounds, it doesn't matter how good a putter you are as you are going to struggle to put a good score together.

In this chapter we are going to discuss the long game and I am going to offer you several thoughts and suggestions that I confidently predict will help you to score better. It is not my intention to tell you how to swing the club as this is discussed in another section of the book, but I will offer you guidance on the type of equipment you should use.

Below: Setting up for a drive with the correct alignment through the shoulders, hips, knees and feet. A little more flexation of the knees, a problem in Seniors, is needed to make it really spark.

Equipment

At any stage in your golfing life, no matter how young or old you are, you must use the clubs that are best suited to your individual physique. To most golfers a golf club is a golf club. One 5 iron looks much the same as another 5 iron: they both have a shaft, they both have a grip and they both have a head. However, there are many ways in which one set of clubs can differ from another set. Shaft length, weight, swingweight (balance), shaft flex, lie, grip thickness and loft all have to be taken into account.

As you get older you can no longer handle the type of clubs that suited you when you were younger. From my experience, most senior golfers use clubs that are too heavy and have too stiff a shaft. This being the case, how can you possibly expect to play to your full potential?

I have often heard people say that clubs do not make any difference at all to anyone's performance. Phrases such as 'a bad workman blames his tools' readily spring to mind, or 'I once used to be able to play quite well with this set', or the one that makes me smile the most: 'You could give Jack Nicklaus any old set of clubs and he would still get round under par!' I can assure you that I could put a set of clubs in Mr Nicklaus's bag that would give him no chance of breaking par. In saying this I mean no disrespect to Jack, who is probably the greatest golfer the world has ever seen. I simply use this as an illustration that to play to your full potential you and Jack Nicklaus must use the equipment that is best suited to your personal physique and swing.

As we get older we must consider four very important aspects of golf club design: the lie, weight, shaft and grip.

Lie

The lie of the club is the angle at which the shaft leaves the head when the sole is sitting flat on the ground. A club that is too 'flat' lying will tend to hit the ball to the right, whereas one that lies too upright will, conversely, tend to hit the ball to the left.

You can usually tell if your irons sit correctly by looking at your divots. If the depth of the divot is uniform, then all is well. If the toe side of the divot is deeper than the heel and if the toe of the club appears to have made contact with the ground before the heel, then the club is too flat lying for your swing. The reverse also applies: if the heel appears to have entered the ground first and if the heel side of the divot is deeper, the lie is too upright for your swing. In either event an incorrect lie can have a pretty disastrous effect on the direction in which you hit the ball, particularly on your long irons.

The correct lie

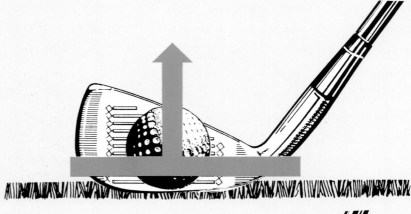

Correct lie
This is the correct lie
for a straight shot
with a uniform divot.

Lie too upright
The deep heel side of
the divot. The ball
will be hit to the left
of the target.

Lie too flat
Deep toe side of divot.
The ball will be hit to
the right of target.

Above: The lie of this 5 iron is too flat for this golfer, but he is trying to make it normal. He is very crouched and his posture is wrong. He is too far from the ball and adjusting his swing to the club instead of his club to the swing. Ask your professional to check the lie of your clubs; they can be adjusted to suit you personally.

Head design: irons

When you are browsing around your golf professional's shop you will see many different head shapes on the sets of irons, but they are basically all variations on two themes.

Firstly, there is what I class as the blade head. This is a straightforward design that tapers from the sole to the top edge. This style has been around since golf first began and is favoured generally by the low-handicap and professional player.

The second category is the cavity back or 'game improvement' design, where basically the weight has been removed from the hitting area, generally increasing the weight of the sole and also the heel and toe area. This design feature effectively assists the slight mis-hit, encouraging the thin shot to climb in the air, and the shot hit to the left or right of centre to go further and straighter than a similar strike with a blade-headed club.

In short, I would strongly advise the use of this latter head design to virtually all players.

Above: The design of club heads has changed over the last decade to create a variety of head designs. These are the two most common variations for irons: the blade head and cavity back head.

Head design: woods

With regard to woods, the metal head varieties are definitely advisable as they are more forgiving than their wooden counterparts. A wooden head is a solid block with a pronounced 'sweet spot' in the centre of the face. However, the metal-headed club is hollow with the weight therefore concentrated around the perimeter of the club face, enabling the off-centre strike to carry further and fly straighter than its wooden counterpart.

Above: A traditional persimmon head. This sort of club head is usually created by hand by only a few skilled craftsmen.

Above: Metal-headed drivers have an enlarged sweet spot. The weight is concentrated around the perimeter of the face to carry the ball further.

Utility clubs

This is a term given to odd clubs that are designed with a specific job in mind and which are not found in conventional sets of clubs. They are also many and varied and most are of use to the senior golfer. Chippers, backspin wedges and lofted woods all fall into this category. I will not dwell on the pros and cons of these clubs here as their uses are explained elsewhere.

Weight

The weight of a golf club is particularly important to the more senior golfer. Whether we like it or not, it is inevitable that the older we get the weaker we get. You may not want to admit this but it is a medical fact! Therefore, it is obvious that you will not be able to swing the club as fast as you could in your youth. However, you will find that you can swing a light club faster than a heavy club. This is an important factor to bear in mind with particular relevance to the senior's long game. You will generate more club head speed and therefore hit the ball further with a lightweight club.

This argument is clear for all to understand, so the obvious remedy you might think is to make your woods lighter. Your professional can do this for you by removing weight from the head of your wooden-headed clubs, although this is not usually possible with the modern metal heads. However, here comes the snag – this is not the answer. By removing a reasonable amount of weight from the head you may end up with a lighter club but you will have destroyed its 'balance'. As you swing the

Equipment tip

In his heyday, the great Irish champion Fred Daly used a driver weighing 15.75 ounces. The driver I use weighs 11.3 ounces.

club, you will have lost the 'feel' of the head, and this should not be sacrificed. If anything, you want to create a greater awareness of the club head, particularly with the longer-shafted clubs.

Shaft

This brings me to the most important part of the golf club with relevance to its suitability to the individual. With the advancement of technology the new lightweight steel, graphite and titanium shafts are far lighter than their normal counterparts. This enables us to obtain a lighter overall weight but still retain, or if anything enhance, the feel of the head.

Now we are getting closer to the correct club for the senior golfer to use. As we have already established, we can create more club head speed with a lighter club, and even more club head acceleration can be achieved with the correct shaft flex. By and large the older golfer can achieve maximum club head speed with a whippier shaft. I would strongly advise you to consult your Club Professional on this aspect. He will be able to offer you his skilled advice and may even have a trial club with which you may experiment.

Grip

Many newly retired golfers come to me saying that they wish to buy themselves a retirement present, as they are now going to have a lot more time to play golf. In seeking

Pointer tip

Always keep your hands warm. As you get older your circulation will not be as good as it used to be. A good tip in winter is to soak your hands in warm water before going out to play. When the weather is cold, make use of any of the various hand-warmer products that are on the market. If your hands are cold you will lose the feel of the club.

Above: You can see that the shaft of the man's club is much longer with a thicker grip than that of the lady's club, which tends to have a lighter more flexible shaft and is usually an inch shorter.

my advice they often ask, now that they are getting older, would ladies' clubs be a good idea?

In some ways, this is a good thought, in as much as a lady's club is lighter and more flexible in the shaft than a standard man's club. However, there are two drawbacks to a man using a lady's club, the first being the shaft length. A lady's club is normally an inch shorter than a man's, and although this does not sound much, it does effectively reduce the arc of the swing with the resulting loss in distance. Also, the taller individual will struggle with the shorter club. The second drawback is the grip thickness: ladies' grips are appreciably thinner than those fitted to a man's club.

This may be all right for those with fairly small hands, but it is generally unacceptable, particularly for the older golfer whose grip on the club is not as firm as it used to be. In fact, for those of you who may

be unfortunate enough to suffer from arthritis or similar complaints, I would strongly recommend a thicker than standard grip. A standard man's grip can be under-packed to make it thicker, or there are oversize grips specifically manufactured called 'Jumbo' or 'Arthritic' grips.

I hope that I have opened your eyes to some of the club design concepts that are

Left: If the grip is too thin, the fingers are not round the club but digging into the pad of the left thumb. This can cause lack of control and will adversely affect your swing. Below: The jumbo grip is perfect for people with large hands and is often recommended for golfers with arthritic or weak hands as it gives you extra control.

available to assist you, the senior golfer, to retain, if not hopefully improve, your long game. Making sure that you use the equipment that is best suited to you is no guarantee that you will become a better golfer, but mark my words it will certainly help!

Improving your long game

Now let us improve your long game still further. We can do this quite simply and with often surprising results to your score and handicap without actually altering your swing at all. What you have to do is to improve your thinking. You must improve your approach to tackling the problems that lie in wait for you on your trip around the golf course. This is called 'course management' and there are several aspects to this subject.

Basically, the whole concept relates to how you can best get the ball from point A (the tee) to point B (the hole) in the fewest number of shots. To achieve this it is essential that you avoid all obstacles that are put in your way!

In short, you must try to get inside the mind of the architect who designed the course you are playing. Over the years, this profession has evolved a particularly devious

Below: Modern golf course architects often require thousands of tons of soil to be moved to accommodate their designs. Here we can see tees and greens that have been cut into the side of a hill at St Mellion.

and sadistic group of human beings. It is their job to present you with a challenge: an examination that you must pass with flying colours to card a good score. I can assure you that there is a lot more to the long game than just being able to hit the ball. The course designer has a veritable arsenal at his disposal to combat your attack on his course: rough, trees, sand bunkers, streams, ditches, ponds and out-of-bounds areas are all part of his defences. It is your task to avoid these with each shot you play. It is my task here to make you aware of this and assist you through the minefield.

Distances

The modern Golf Professional treats the subject of course management as a science. He, or should I say his caddy, knows the exact distance to the hole from any given spot on the fairway and, equally to the point, he knows how far any hazard is from the tee. Most golf courses have yardage charts that show distances to or from various landmarks,

but you can always make your own. To manage your way around the course this is very important. However, to gain any benefit you must also know how far you can hit with your various clubs. It is well worth spending a while on the practice ground to gain this information. With this new-found knowledge you are now in a position to plan your way around any golf course.

Above: The yardage chart not only shows you the length but also the shape of the hole and problems such as trees and bunkers. This helps to form an accurate picture of how you are going to play it.

Driving

Which club should you use to play your first shot on each hole? Discounting the par 3 holes, there are probably thirteen or fourteen holes on most courses where you cannot reach the green with your tee shot. It is generally assumed that on these holes you should use the driver (No. 1 wood); this is the club that will hit the ball further than any other club in your bag. It has the longest shaft and the straightest face, and therefore it is designed to hit the ball the furthest. However, because it does have the longest shaft and the straightest face, it is also the most difficult club in the bag with which to produce consistently good shots.

I often hear the more senior golfers among us saying that they hit the ball just as far with their 3 wood as they do with their driver. This I can understand because the short shaft makes the 3 wood easier to control; the heavier head (yes, the driver is the lightest of the woods) gives more 'feel'; and the extra loft encourages the ball into the air better and helps to reduce side-spin.

If you struggle with a No. 1 wood, let me suggest you ask your Professional to check its loft. Although a No. 2 wood is

Below: The 3 wood and 1 wood show the different tee heights and difference between the club face lofts. Note that the ball is teed lower with the lofted 3 wood, almost to the height of a good fairway lie.

seldom produced by most manufacturers these days, many do make a No. 1 wood with a 12 degree loft (equivalent to a No. 2 wood). This basically makes the club easier to use, but because it still has the shaft length of a driver, will hit the ball further than the No. 3 wood.

If you are convinced that the 3 wood is the club for you, far be it for me to talk you out of using it for those tee shots where you require maximum distance. However, I want you to realise that you do not always require maximum distance. Whether you use a 1

wood or a 3 wood, if you are like the vast majority of golfers throughout the world, when you step onto the tee of a par 4 or par 5 hole off will come the head cover of your 'trusty' driving club. However, this is often a big mistake.

Be aware, each time you stand on the tee, that no matter what hole you are

Below: Simon Lloyd is about to hit an iron for safety at St Mellion's fearsome 3rd hole. You can see the contours of the land and the large chasm to the right of the fairway. This is where safety play comes in.

playing, the most important thing you have to achieve is to hit the fairway. Fair enough if you are presented with a nice wide open fairway, with only light rough on either side, then by all means use your driver. However, if the fairway narrows at your driving range (say, 200 yards) it is often sensible to lay up short by using a shorter club and hitting into the wider part of the fairway. By doing this you are obviously giving away distance but you will be playing your second shot from

Above: Our cameraman has excelled himself! One player has already hit the fairway with a 5 wood. The second player, attempting a big hit with a driver, has hit the ball further but has sliced it and we can see his ball, which is about to hop into the fairway bunker.

the fairway rather than a bunker or deep rough or, worse still, finding your ball out-of-bounds or in a water hazard, and having to suffer the appropriate penalty.

Beware of fairway bunkers! The course architect has not made use of this type of hazard for aesthetic purposes; he has placed them strategically to try to catch your tee shot. Discover how far that bunker is from the tee. Let us say that a fairway bunker is situated at 180 yards. You may well be able to drive 200 yards, but can you carry the ball far enough through the air to clear the bunker? In short, think 'safety first' and ensure that you get your tee shot into play.

The fairway woods

As we advance in years, we find that we use the fairway woods more and more. This is due to the fact that as we lose distance the holes begin to play longer, therefore requiring more use of the heavy artillery. Just as we have been discussing the need for good thinking and selective use of the driver off the tee, beware of over-use of the fairway wood for your second shot. If your ball is sitting well and you estimate you have a good chance of reaching the green with your 3 wood, then have a go by all means. However, if your very best shot is going to leave you some way short of the green, you should seriously question the wisdom of using that club. The fairways on many golf holes narrow jut short of the green either due to skilfully placed bunkers, an encroaching tree or even a water hazard, so if the very best result achieveable with a 3 wood is to leave a thirty or forty yard pitch shot, why risk putting the ball in trouble when a 5 iron

Left: A tight lie for a 3 wood. With this lie, especially if the ground is hard, it is always a risky shot. If you're going to try this shot, position the ball slightly further back in the stance. Concentrate on your swing and rhythm rather than on hitting the ball out of a bad lie.

Above: This photograph shows the set up for a 3 wood. Note that the golfer is positioned slightly further away from the ball than is the case for an iron. He is set up in a nice, relaxed position ready to hit the ball further along the fairway.

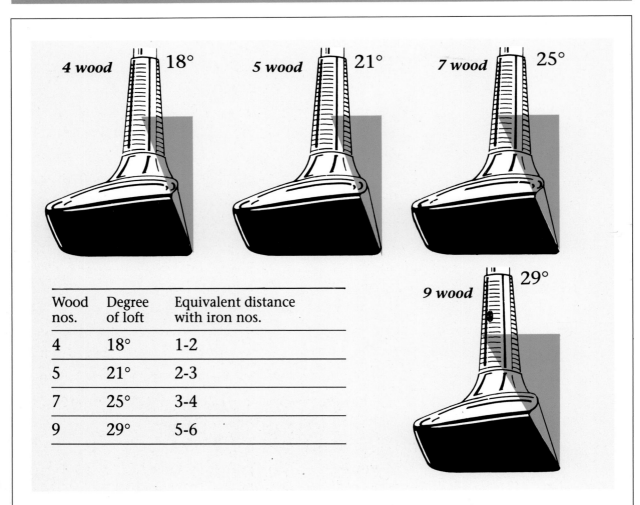

Wood nos.	Degree of loft	Equivalent distance with iron nos.
4	18°	1-2
5	21°	2-3
7	25°	3-4
9	29°	5-6

second shot should place the ball in a good position to leave an easy 9 iron to the green?

When playing the fairway woods do not be too ambitious. If, as you address the ball with your 3 wood, you start thinking that the lie is a little bare and wonder if you will be able to get the ball airborne properly – stop. Think again and use a more lofted club. You will almost certainly hit a better shot and thereby gain just as much distance.

The long irons

There is a lovely story that has been attributed to many well-known Professionals, but which I think originated with Sam Snead. He was giving a golfing clinic one day and, after enthralling the crowd with his shot-making expertise and his comments on the golf swing, one of the more senior members of his audience asked: "Mr Snead, how can I get my 3 iron to stop quicker?" Sam politely enquired: "How far do you hit your 3 iron?" "Oh, about 160 yards." "In that case, what on earth do you want it to stop for?" came the reply.

That little story never ceases to make me smile, but it is pertinent to the subject of the long iron. Have you noticed as the years go by how your 3, 4 and 5 irons all seem to make the ball travel about the same distance? Or at least how there is very little difference in the distance they carry through the air?

The faster the club head travels the more backspin it imparts on the ball and the higher the ball will climb and therefore stay in the air longer. However, as we get older and can no longer generate the club head speed of the younger, stronger players, so less backspin is imparted, resulting in lower shots with shorter carry. As this happens, so a large gap starts to open up between your woods and your irons. Let us say that your well struck 5 wood will carry 170 yards through the air and stop reasonably quickly.

However, your well struck 3 iron (the 5 wood's nearest neighbour in the set) will probably only carry 140 yards and then run forward. The relative distances the two shots have covered are more or less correct, the 5 wood being ten to fifteen yards longer than the 3 iron. However, there is a thirty-yard gap between their respective 'carries'.

Let us assume that you are faced with a shot that requires you to carry the ball 150 yards over a pond to a fairly small green; which club should you use? Your 3 or 4 iron would go the distance but will not carry far enough to clear the water; and your 5 wood will carry clear over the back of the green.

This is where the golf club manufacturers again have come to the aid of the senior golfer. It is possible to obtain No. 6 and No. 7 woods. In fact, some manufacturers make No. 9 and No. 11 and I have even seen a No. 13 wood!

A 6 wood will therefore hit a higher, shorter shot than a 5 wood. In other words, hitting the ball about the same overall distance as a 3 iron but with greater carry. A 7 wood will, in turn, hit about the same distance as a 4 iron but again with greater carry.

So what I am suggesting is that unless you feel particularly happy with your long irons, it is well worth replacing them with an extra lofted wood thereby filling that hole in

Continued on page 69

Rough tip

Although the 5 and 6 woods are far more effective than a long iron for the senior golfer to gain distance from light rough, do not be too ambitious. Use a club with which you are sure you can get the ball back on to the fairway.

Right and below: A grassy lie just off the fairway is safe to use a wood provided that you can set the club to contact below the equator of the ball.

Left: A modern 7 wood has been designed to help people get the ball into the air from the fairway. It is approximately the same loft as a 4 iron. A 7 wood is most useful for tight lies, but the 4 iron with its cutting blade is still favourite.

Woods versus irons

You are faced with a shot of 150 yards over a pond to a small green. A 4 iron will go the distance but will not clear the water. A 6 wood will hit a higher shorter shot. A 5 wood will carry clear over the back of the green. So play safe and use an extra lofted wood rather than your long irons. The 6 wood will give you the high carrying shot.

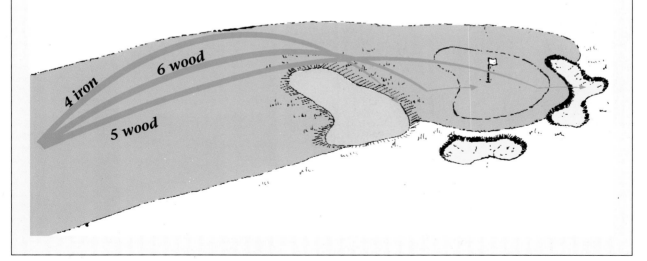

your bag. Lee Trevino has recently started to use a 6 wood, and I feel that this proves my point. Even Lee Trevino, regarded as one of the greatest manufacturers of shots the game has ever seen, has discovered that, now he is getting older, the 6 wood helps him to achieve that high-carrying shot with greater ease than a long iron.

While talking of Lee Trevino, who is not only a great manufacturer of shots but also a master at thinking his way around a golf course, I would mention one occasion when even he got it wrong. While playing in the one British Open at Birkdale, he made an

Swing speed tip

One of Gary Player's sayings was "Swing fast – won't last, Swing slow – take the dough!" Think about it!

awful mess of the seventeenth hole. This is a par 5 hole which to stand a chance of reaching the green in two shots and thereby hopefully achieving a birdie, requires a long accurate drive between two giant sand dunes. Trevino hooked his drive and got into all sorts of trouble, eventually costing him any chance of the Championship.

This sequence demonstrates the concept of turning and unturning, swinging the extended arms back and through the hitting area. Note the turning of the shoulders and the sympathetic movements as the wrists start to cock.

Dangerous par 4's

St Mellion's par 4 3rd hole is relatively short, measuring 356 yds from the Medal tee. However, the hole is deceptive and fraught with danger.

Any shot missing the fairway to the right falls into a steep grassy ravine, probably never to be seen again. A ball missing the fairway left will lodge in thick rough in a steep bank that descends to the edge of the fairway.

Although two of your very best shots may find the greens if you stray slightly off-line, the result could prove to be a real card wrecker.

However, a long iron or lofted wood should find the fairway at about 150-160 yards from the tee. A second shot with a 5 iron should cover another 140 yards into the wide part of the fairway, comfortably short of the green-side bunkers leaving you with a 50-60 yard pitch to the green. This allows two putts for an easy 5 or the possibility of one putt for a more desirable par 4.

Below: The third hole at St Mellion from the tee. There is a chance of a pitch and a putt for 4 if you play safely. Play a good pitch shot to a fairway lie rather than risk ending up in a bunker or a sloping lie.

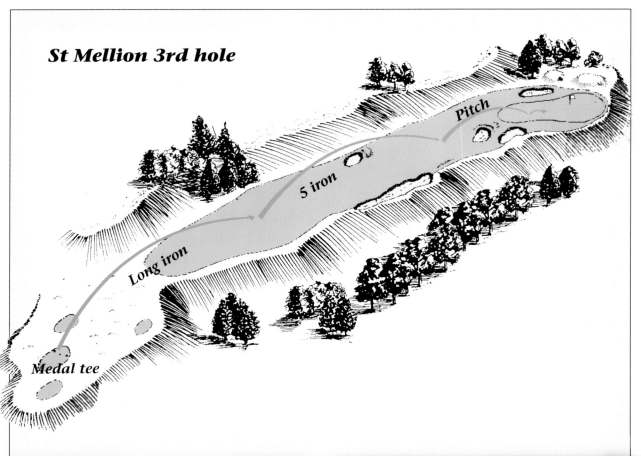

St Mellion 3rd hole

Pitch

5 iron

Long iron

Medal tee

Left: View along the length of the 3rd hole fairway. Above: A bird's eye view of the landing area for the second shot.

I only cite this instance because I also saw the great South African golfer Bobby Locke play the same hole. He used a 4 iron from the tee followed by a 3 wood, then hit an 8 iron onto the green and holed the putt for his birdie! Bobby Locke had eliminated all the dangers that the hole presented. As it was he got his birdie but the worst that could have happened was a par.

So as you stand on each tee, plan out the hole. Your aim is to avoid trouble, not to flirt with danger. Don't attempt any shot that requires 100 per cent perfection – play the percentages. Remember that there is no point getting older if you don't get wiser.

Although at the beginning of this chapter I said that I would not actually discuss the methods used to address the ball and swing the club, I cannot resist offering one or two thoughts that I feel are particularly relevant to the older player when using the longer shafted clubs.

Firstly, never forget that the movement we use to strike the golf ball is called a golf *swing*. *Swing* is the operative word; it is not called a golf hit or a golf thrash or a golf swipe but it is called a golf *swing*. We must *swing* the club back and through the ball.

The body should be encouraged to turn and unturn allowing the extended arms to swing back *and* through the hitting area which, in turn, assists the club head to describe as wide an arc as possible. Awareness of the club head is essential and I cannot over-emphasize my earlier comments about equipment.

Maybe you don't hit the ball as far as the youngsters. You must accept this and not try to keep up with them. The harder you try to hit the ball the more likely you are to miss-time the swing and mishit the ball resulting in the complete opposite to what you were trying to achieve.

Develop this good swinging action and couple it with a good rhythm and you will be surprised at the distance you can achieve.

The short game

By Tony Moore

When I started to co-write this book, with the emphasis on instruction for the senior golfer, I thought that I had better do a little research into the subject. So I asked someone who I considered to be one of our more Senior Club members at St Mellion, whom I knew had been playing golf for a long time, the differences and difficulties he had experienced now that he was not so young as he used to be.

What an interesting chat we had. He spoke about loss of length: how he could no longer reach this hole and that hole in two shots. He felt that the rough must now be thicker because he could not get the ball out of it anywhere near as well as he used to. He went on to say how his short game had gradually deteriorated, especially his pitch shots over bunkers which he now duffed into the bunker far more often than ever before. Finally, his putting, particularly the short putts, was now nothing short of embarrassing. He felt much more tired at the end of a round than he could ever remember and, of course, his handicap, despite increasing over the last few years, had not been played to for ages.

Finally I asked him his age and to my horror discovered that this 'elderly gentleman' was only five years older than me. I swiftly concluded that he must have led a very hard life! However, sitting at home in front of the fire that night, in my slippers,

sipping a hot drink, I started to realise that a lot of what he said had struck a chord. I did tire more easily these days. Even though I was never a particularly long hitter, I was getting even shorter. My short game was losing its edge, and as for those three-foot putts, I had been missing those with monotonous regularity for several years.

So it comes to us all in time, but, as far as golf is concerned, do not despair. What other sport can you continue to play into your seventies, eighties and beyond, which is played in pleasant, often glorious, surroundings, in good company and in which you can still be competitive?

It is important to realise your limitations and adapt accordingly. I hope that you will glean some assistance from the following pages. Obviously, whether you are seventeen or seventy, certain aspects and techniques of the game will remain the same. However, I hope to guide you into playing certain shots in maybe a slightly modified way and to encourage you into using specific thought patterns that will prevent you from unnecessarily frittering too many shots away and will help you to save a few shots as well.

In my opinion, the most fascinating, not to mention rewarding, part of the game of golf is the short game. This is the general heading given to all shots played from within, let us say, 50 yards of the hole and encompassing putting, chipping, pitching

and bunker shots. This is the area of the game where countless shots can be saved; where a potentially bad round of golf can be turned into a good score, or a good round of golf can become an exceptional one. The real beauty of this part of the game is that young and old, male and female, can all compete on level terms. Physical strength and ability do not play a part in this department of the game. I am often told by young Club members how they played against one of the Veterans who has probably been drawing his old age pension for more years than he cares to remember, and how they were taking a shot less than him to reach the green but how he kept chipping and single putting, thereby halving the hole with them.

Even with this in mind, as you get older it must not be assumed that it is a God-given right that your short game automatically improves – far from it. A sound knowledge and understanding of the various techniques, correct club selection and plenty of practice are all required.

With the advancement of old age and the consequent gradual loss of physical strength and agility, it is inevitable that fewer and fewer greens will be hit in regulation figures. This is either because the green simply cannot be reached as it is out of range, or because such a long club is required that accuracy cannot be guaranteed. Because

of this, logic dictates that as you get older, you should become increasingly dependent upon the short game.

With this in mind, let us first consider the shot that you will be confronted with many times during a round of golf; this is the shot where the ball is lying on the fairway within 20-30 yards of the hole. How best can you get that ball into the hole in two shots?

Practice drill

The first problem to solve is which club should you use? To give you an idea of how to answer this question I would ask you to perform a simple exercise next time you are at your Golf Club. Take six white balls and six yellow balls to the practice green. Firstly bowl the white balls underarm along the ground towards the hole, and then throw the yellow balls up into the air at the hole. I will have a little bet that the white balls (the low running action) will be clustered closer to the hole than the yellow (high lobbing action). This exercise tells us that a low running shot is easier to control and easier to reproduce.

Bearing this is mind, when I am discussing these shots with my pupils who are struggling with this part of the game, be they young or old, I suggest a choice of three shots which are outlined here.

The running shot

Your first thought should *always* be: "Is it feasible to use my putter?" The putter is not restricted purely to work on the green. Using the putter from off the green may be frowned upon in some quarters, but is, in fact, a perfectly legitimate shot, not to mention an excellent addition to your stroke-saving armoury! Ask yourself the question: "How often do I top a putt or stub the ground before I make contact with the ball?" I am sure that the answer will be that you very rarely do either. In addition, as we have already demonstrated, it is far easier to judge the running shot, commonly called the 'Texas wedge'.

The chip shot

So the first thought must always be the putter. You may feel that this is not practical as you cannot judge accurately the pace with a putter because you are either too far away from the hole, or the fairway grass is too long or too wet. If the putter is eliminated, your second choice should be the closest relation to a putt. A shot that lifts slightly, lands on the edge of the green and runs forwards towards the hole is known as the chip shot.

Chipping tip

Never try to chip with a straight-faced club from the rough: too much grass will be sandwiched between the club face and the ball. Use a wedge to pitch the ball; the more descending blow will make contact with less grass and the 'sharper' leading edge effectively will cut through the grass better.

I would suggest that you start by concentrating on using a 5 or 6 iron to play the shot. By doing this you will become familiar with the shot that this club produces and should start fairly quickly to produce repetitive results. As you gain confidence in this shot you may start to experiment with other clubs. For instance, if the ground is a bit rough, or there is an undulation where you plan to land your 6 iron, you may decide to select an 8 or 9 which you can hit harder to carry the ball further through the air and not run quite so far.

The pitch shot

It is not always practical to play this low-running shot. There may be a bunker or steep grassy bank between you and the hole which necessitates a high shot to negotiate the obstacle and stop quickly before running right over the green. For this type of shot, you must delve deeper into your bag for a pitching wedge or maybe even a sand iron. This shot is called the *pitch shot*.

So when you have missed the green these are the three basic types of shots available to you. Before moving on to

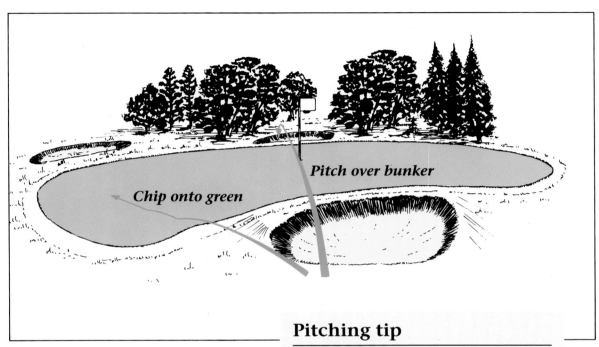

Pitch over bunker

Chip onto green

Opposite: The chipper and the 6 iron both have the same loft. However, the chipper has a more upright lie enabling it to be swung like a putter in more of a pendulum movement. The Senior may feel safer with the chipper as it helps to instill confidence.

Pitching tip

Don't try the impossible or improbable. Don't try to pitch over a bunker from a really tight lie to get to a tight pin position. Chip to the side of the bunker to another part of the green and accept two putts. It seems negative, but beats duffing it into the bunker or thinning it over the green which is probably what would happen.

describe the techniques required to play these shots, I will just mention one other option which, should you really struggle to obtain acceptable, consistent results, may just be of assistance. There is a club available that, for want of a better way of describing it, is basically a putter with the loft of about a 6 iron. This club is called a 'chipper' or a 'jigger' and it sits like a putter. In other words, it has an upright lie which enables the user to adopt his normal putting stance

and stroke, letting the loft of the face lift the ball in the same way as a 6 iron chip shot. This type of club has assisted many people, particularly the elderly who have, over the years, developed very suspect and jerky chipping actions. So if you really are struggling to master the chip shot, ask your Club Professional to show you one.

The chipper stroke

This photographic sequence shows the chipper stroke. This club is a member of the putting family. Set up in the usual way as though you are going to putt. You have chosen to use your chipper because of the rough grass between you and the green; the loft on the chipper will take care of this. You usually play this shot from just off the green so, as with a putt, you just lengthen the backswing. Don't be tempted into making a hit at the ball; remember that it is a putting stroke throughout. Keep the body still on the downward movement; the hands and arms make the movement into and through the ball. Keep the head still throughout the shot. Seniors can also use the chipper for longer distances when they're not sure of their more lofted clubs.

If there are no bunkers in the way, you can use the chipper from 30 to 40 yards. The length of the shaft gives you the finesse and the feel of a putter.

The Texas wedge

As I have already stated, the putter should be your first thought when deciding how best to get your ball close to the hole from off the green. I will discuss the putting stroke later on, but I will mention a couple of additional points that I feel are pertinent to using the putter from off the green. Firstly, this shot is likely to be a longer putt than the ones with which you are normally faced, so avoid the temptation to hit or stab at the ball in an effort to negotiate the additional yardage. To help you prevent this happening, try to feel that you are standing taller as you address the ball and encourage a smooth pendulum stroke back *and* through the ball.

On any long putt, whether from on or

This sequence shows the Texas wedge in action. It is often used by good putters who have trouble with long off-the-green shots and very hard ground, e.g. bare lies just off the green. The ball is positioned opposite the inside of the left foot. Make a stiff-wristed pendulum action back and through the ball. The follow through should be at least as long as the backswing.

off the green, virtually all golfers will leave the ball short of the hole. Analyse your next few rounds and I am sure you will be no exception. Other than stating the obvious by saying hit the ball harder than you think, it is hard to help you here! It may be worthwhile imagining that the hole is three or four feet further away than it really is. In a more technical vein, make sure that you swing the putter head through the ball

properly: follow through. This will encourage acceleration and, more to the point, discourage the tendency to slow down at impact.

One final word on this shot: if you find yourself undecided as to how hard to hit the ball to compensate for the length of the fairway grass between your ball and the green, put the putter back in the bag and recognise that you have selected the wrong club!

Executing the chip shot

Until you have gained a good degree of confidence and consistency in this shot, I would suggest that you stick with one club; let us say the number 6 iron. Remember that we are trying to produce a low shot that will run forward when it lands. Also remember that your seniority does not prevent you from mastering this shot and becoming just as proficient as those young tigers at your Club!

As in all shots, the first thing to do is to aim the club face in the direction you want the ball to go. Make sure that you line up with the bottom edge and not the top edge of the club. Lining up with the top edge will effectively close the club face and most certainly pull the ball to the left of the intended line. While on the subject of club head alignment, I would just mention that we all assume that we line the club head up correctly with the target, but with many golfers this is a false assumption. You can check this easily for yourself by laying a club on the ground parallel to the intended line of fire and seeing if the leading edge of the blade (bottom edge) is at right angles to this club. Over the years I have noticed that many senior golfers have a problem with this seemingly simple task, so take time to check and practise with the aid of this second club.

Having lined the club head up with the intended line, grip the club as for a full shot except that you should hold the grip of the club lower down than usual. This is particularly relevant for shorter seniors and ladies as it effectively shortens the shaft allowing for more control. The hands should be positioned ahead of the club head so that the back of the left hand is level with the crease on your left trouser leg.

You are now ready to form your stance. This is an area in which you are going to make several changes from the stance you adopt for a full shot. A line drawn across the toe caps of both feet, and a line across the hips should point slightly to the left of the target. However, the shoulders should be kept square to the intended line – this is called an open stance. The ball should be positioned opposite the inside of the left heel and the weight should favour the left foot in approximately a 60:40 ratio.

We adopt the open stance with feet and hips because as there is little or no body

Opposite: The address position for the chip shot. Note the open stance where the shoulders are kept square to the intended line. The ball is positioned opposite the inside of the left heel with the weight slightly favouring the left foot to encourage it to stay there at impact with the ball.

turn on the backswing, and, more to the point, no unturn on the downswing, the left hip is already slightly out of the way before you swing, thereby allowing the follow through not to be restricted.

Because there is little or no weight transfer in this shot, you start by standing with more weight on the left foot to encourage it to remain on that foot at impact, which, in turn, encourages the club head to reach the bottom of its arc opposite the left foot. In other words, the bottom of the swing should occur at or just after impact with the ball.

The stroke itself should be made with a swinging movement of the arms, hands and club. They should move backwards and forwards together in a pendulum action; there should be no wrist action involved in this shot. In fact, you can think of it as an extension of the putting stroke. The weight should remain on the left foot thereby encouraging the base of the arc of the swing to occur at or marginally after contact with the ball. This will allow the loft of the club head to lift the ball. Under no circumstances should you attempt consciously to scoop or flick the ball into the air.

I have already likened the swinging action for this shot to that of a pendulum. Remember that however far a pendulum swings in one direction, it will swing the same distance in the other direction, so ensure that the follow through is at least as

long as the backswing.

Take time to practise and get to grips with this simple shot. It really is a great stroke saver for golfers of all ages, but in particular for those seniors whose co-ordination and 'eye for a ball' may not be quite as good as it was. You will notice while practising that the slight mishit still finishes reasonably close to the hole, unlike a comparable mishit with one of the wedges, the use of which we will now discuss.

Opposite: The weight is on the left foot, the ball is opposite the left heel, and the left hand is level with the trouser crease. Above: The backswing is firm-wristed and the weight remains favouring the left foot, encouraging the club head to reach the bottom of its arc opposite the left foot, at or just after impact. Above right: Just after impact, the wrist stays firm, and the weight on the left foot as the club swings through.

Chipping tip

If faced with a shot that has to go up and over a mown bank, play the ball further back in the stance with, say, a 6 iron as described, but hood (close) the face and try to hit the ball with a slight in-to-out swing. This will impart very little backspin, encouraging the ball to run up the bank. Also try to land the ball and therefore get it running before the bank. A ball pitched into the bank will often not run forwards.

Left: Playing a shot from off the green with a sloping bank in front and little room to work with to get on to the green. Play this shot with a 5 or 6 iron. Position the ball slightly backwards in the stance, hooding (de-lofting) the blade a little. This gives the running movement which enables the ball to climb the bank and keep it rolling the short distance needed on the green.

Chipping tip

Pick a spot where you want the ball to land. Visualize the shot landing on that particular spot and running up to the hole. Have a clear picture, not just a vague thought, of hitting towards the hole.

Above: It is most important when you are chipping or pitching to visualize the shot and where you're going to chip or pitch the ball. Take your line, cutting out the pin altogether. Concentrate only on where you want the ball to land and the roll. You should already have taken the roll to the pin into account so there is no need to dwell on the pin itself. This will just be distracting for you.

Executing the pitch shot

I would suggest that the senior golfer attempts this shot only when he or she has no alternative: in other words, when faced with a shot that must clear a bunker, stream or similar obstruction, and stop quickly.

In my opinion the wedges are the most over-used clubs in the handicap golfer's bag. In the forty odd years that I have been playing golf as a Professional I have played with thousands of handicap golfers who, as soon as they are faced with anything other than a full shot, immediately reach for a wedge. At least seventy-five per cent of the time they should have been attempting the chip shot with a less lofted straight-faced club.

When playing the pitch shot, you are trying to lift the ball quickly and eliminate as much forward run as possible. Therefore the sand iron, the most lofted club in the bag, is the obvious choice for this shot. However, first you must discover whether *your* sand iron is suitable as not all of them sit correctly for a pitch off turf, particularly from a tight lie. Take your address position, which I will describe later, on a hard surface (a concrete path or a lino floor). Now look to see if the leading edge of your sand iron is raised off the ground. All sand irons are designed in such a way that the back edge of the flange or sole is proud of the front edge, the reason for which I will discuss in the section on

Pitching tip

As the years go by, those pitch shots are just not going to stop as quickly as they did. Allow for this.

bunker shots. Although this design feature is beneficial in playing from sand, it can, if too exaggerated, be detrimental for a pitch off turf. Club manufacturers have different ideas as to the amount of 'bounce', the word given to this design feature, that they incorporate into their sand irons. If the front edge is too raised, the back of the sole will tend to strike the ground too early and make the club bounce into the ball resulting in a thinned shot which will not lift sufficiently and definitely will not stop quickly enough.

I would suggest that if the front edge of your sand iron is raised by one-eighth of an inch or more, you restrict its use to sand shots and only attempt a pitch shot with it if you feel that there is a reasonable amount of grass under the ball. Instead, use your pitching wedge or ask your Professional to show you one of a multitude of utility wedges that are now on the market and have less exaggerated sole features, but still possess the loft of a sand iron. Should you decide to purchase this additional piece of equipment it is worth considering a club with 'square' grooves. These grooves are box-shaped rather

than 'V'-shaped and definitely assist in imparting backspin on the ball. This will be a distinct advantage to the senior golfer who will find that as the years go by, due to lack of acceleration and crispness of strike, any assistance in imparting backspin should be grasped with both hands.

The set up for the pitch shot, whether

Above left: The address position for the pitch shot is virtually identical to the one you adopt for the chip shot. Above: The address position for a pitch with a sand iron over a bunker. Note the player's exaggerated open stance.

using the sand iron or pitching wedge should be similar to that for the chip shot, although the open stance concept should be slightly more exaggerated. An additional alteration, although not essential, but in my opinion very helpful in gaining extra height on the shot, concerns the grip. While ensuring that the club face remains facing the target, turn your left hand to the left until only one knuckle is visible and your left thumb is positioned on the top of the grip rather than slightly to the right of centre. You must ensure that the back of the left hand is level with the left trouser crease.

Before you even start to think of the swing, it is very important to realise that the club head must be travelling faster to hit this shot a given distance compared with a chip

shot of the same distance. Simple physics dictates that the greater the loft on the club face the higher the percentage of energy created by the swing used in lifting the ball, and the lower the percentage in driving it forward.

Below: The backswing for the pitch shot. Note the slight hingeing of the wrists to create a steeper descent into the ball, thereby imparting greater backspin Opposite: The wrists are firm, and there's plenty of weight on the left foot as the club head slides under the ball.

Pitching tip

To assist in achieving the feel and action for this shot, practise hitting little pitches. Place the ball on a tee peg no more than half an inch high. Try to cultivate the feeling of trying to nick the peg out of the ground, with the leading edge of the club, while leaving the ball where it is.

Therefore, you are going to make a longer swing for this shot than for a chip shot of the same distance. Although the arms are still going to swing, you may allow the wrists to hinge as you make the backswing. This will encourage a steeper descent into the ball, thereby imparting greater backspin. As we advance in years this hingeing of the wrists should not be too exaggerated as, through loss of agility, you will find it harder and harder to co-ordinate the downswing movement. The downswing should be made by a smooth pull with the left arm down and through the ball. Try to develop the feeling that at impact the back of the left hand is facing the flag, thus holding the club face square. The follow through should finish with the club shaft and both arms pointing towards the flag. I cannot over-emphasise the importance of keeping the left hand and arm swinging into this follow through position. Most people have trouble with this shot as there is a great tendency for the left arm to stop at impact so that the right hand can flick or scoop under the left hand in an attempt to lift the ball into the air. Although the odd good shot will be produced when this happens, it is a very inconsistent action prone to hitting the ground early or thinning the ball.

Opposite: The follow through should be as long as the backswing. Above: The club shaft and both arms should be pointing towards the flag at the end of the follow through. This results from keeping the club face square at impact with the ball.

Putting

If you consider yourself to be a good putter, read no further and turn straight to the next chapter. To a great extent, putting is a mental thing. If you expect to putt well, you will – if you don't, you won't! In the next few pages I will attempt to assist the indifferent to downright bad putter.

"When putting all you have to do is hit the ball in the right direction at the right strength and it will go in the hole." It's as simple as that! This, of course, is said a little bit with tongue in cheek, but, at the end of the day, no matter what type of putter you use, no matter which grip you employ, no matter how you stand, no matter what stroke you make, all you have to do is hit the ball in the right direction and at the right strength. Always keep this in mind.

So what is the correct putting method? Having played with and watched many of the best putters in Professional golf and at Club level, I cannot really say that there is only one way to grip, address or swing.

In my younger days, when I played quite a lot of tournament golf, both in this country and in South Africa, I considered myself a better than average putter. However, as the years have gone by that part of my game has deteriorated gradually and, to be perfectly frank, it is as hard to explain why this should be the case as it is to accept it.

Nevertheless, let me offer you one or two hard and fast rules that I really do consider must be adhered to if you are to stand any chance of developing a consistent stroke and obtaining repetitive results.

Reading the green

Before anything else, you must consider what the ball is going to do after it is struck. Firstly, ask yourself the question: "Is the putt uphill or downhill?" Adjustment to pace must be made always remembering that should you not hole the putt, it is infinitely better to leave yourself a second putt that is uphill. Secondly, you must decide whether you are putting across a slope that, due to gravity, will make the ball curl to the left or

to the right. We call this the 'borrow'. Sometimes, when the slope of the green is quite severe, it is obvious which side you have to aim to start the putt on the uphill side of the hole. However, as we get older, almost inevitably our eyesight is not as good as it was, so we cannot always pick out the more subtle borrows.

I will give you two pieces of advice that I know will help in this respect. The first is to stand behind the ball facing the hole. Now look at the ground to the left and right of the green. If the general terrain is sloping from right to left, you can be pretty sure that the putting surface slopes the same way. The other pointer in this respect should be one of your golden rules – if in doubt, hit it straight. This is particularly relevant on the shorter putts. After all, even if the ball swings up to two inches left or right it should still go into the hole. Also, if you think about it, the dreaded three-putt is virtually never caused because you miss the hole by a long way to the left or right, but almost always because you hit the ball too hard or too soft. I will try to help you with this latter aspect in the practice section of this book.

Putting tip

When replacing your ball on the putting green, take time to point the manufacturer's name towards the intended line. It assists in lining up and encourages the swing to go on the right path.

The grip

Virtually all putters are fitted with a 'reminder' putter grip, i.e. a grip that is shaped in such a way that it has a flat top where the thumbs should sit. Look down the shaft from the butt end of the grip to the head to see if this flat top of the grip is at absolute right angles with the striking face. If it is not, you do not have a chance of putting well! If in doubt, ask your Professional to check for you. If you miss the hole consistently on the same side, a misaligned grip could well be the cause.

How should you hold the club? Well, you can either use the overlapping, double

Right: This is the normal overlapping grip which can be used when you are putting.

overlapping, interlocking, baseball, reverse overlapping, split handed, cack handed or even the broom handle methods! There really is no right or wrong way; use whatever works for you. But if you have an open mind I will give you a couple of options.

Reverse overlap grip

The reverse overlapping grip is the one used by most Tournament Professionals and there is no reason why it should not work for you. It is formed by placing the thumbs on the flat top of the putter grip in such a way that the 'V' formed by the right thumb and

Above: This is the so-called cack-handed grip with the left hand under the right one.

Above: The reverse overlap putting grip which is favoured by most top pros.

forefinger points towards the right shoulder, and the 'V' formed by the left thumb and forefinger points to the left shoulder. Then, rather than overlapping the little finger of the right hand over the index finger of the left hand, as you do if using the Vardon grip for all the other shots, you lay the index finger of the left hand over the little finger of the right hand. This grip does place the hands together in a good solid unit.

Cack handed grip

(left hand under right)

This is an unfortunate name for a grip as it implies awkwardness. Basically, this means gripping with the left hand below the right. By doing this you are trying to encourage the left hand to pull the blade of the club towards the hole, hopefully giving you a good chance of holding the face square to the line of the putt.

Although personally I have not been able to come to terms with this grip and its accompanying different action, I know of a lot of people who have. Bernhard Langer uses a modification of this style very successfully. This is a man who was nearly forced to quit Tournament golf due to being afflicted by the dreaded 'yips'. He now uses a conventional grip for long putts but crosses over for the shorter ones. I feel sure that a lot of senior golfers who are poor putters could benefit from this grip.

Posture

In my opinion, one thing that is essential when putting is to stand in such a way that the eyes are directly over the ball or at least over an extension of the line on which you intend to putt the ball. A simple exercise to check this is to hold a second ball against the top of the nose, between the eyes, and drop

Right: To check whether your head is in the correct position, hold a ball up between your eyes and drop it, keeping your eyes fixed firmly on the ball.

Putting tip

All good putters have a routine. Once you have weighed the putt up, try two practice swings – address the ball – look to the hole twice – focus on the back of the ball – then swing. Go through that same routine, or your variation on it, each time you putt. It must help to breed consistency.

it. If the head is positioned correctly this ball should drop on or directly behind the ball you are about to putt.

If the eyeline is outside the ball, you will tend to pull the ball to the left. Alternatively, if the eyeline is inside the ball, you will tend to push the ball to the right.

Take time to check this on a regular basis; it really is important. In addition, when you are lining the putt up by looking from ball to hole, you are looking straight along the intended line.

The stroke

Although there have been exceptions, virtually all the good putters I have seen use very little, if any, wrist action. The body and head remain perfectly still, and the forearms, wrists, hands and putter swing back and through along the intended line as if one solid unit: a pendulum action.

I have avoided using the phrase 'stiff wristed' as this can imply tension which must be avoided. All the great players maintain that they grip the putter gently – not to be confused with loosely. I am sure that as we get older, and have more than realised that short putts can be missed, we grip the putter more tightly. Think about this

next time you play and try to sense that you are holding a sparrow in your hands. You must hold firmly enough that it cannot

Putting tip

If your eyesight is anything but perfect, have the flag attended on all putts over fifteen feet. Not only does the flag indicate the hole clearly but someone standing next to the flag helps with the distance. This latter point is worth bearing in mind on chip shots too.

escape your grasp, but not so tightly that you will hurt it.

The older player who may have a certain amount of stiffening or arthritis in the finger joints will definitely benefit and get a better 'feel' for this by experimenting with a thicker grip. In doing this it may be that you need to add a little additional weight to the head to retain the original balance. Speak to your Professional about this and I am sure he will advise and assist you.

The senior golfer should beware of the following points, which seem to creep into

This sequence shows the pendulum putting swing; a backwards and forwards movement with the club head travelling along the ball-to-target line.

the older player's putting stroke without him being aware of them.

Be careful that you do not make the backswing too short. I am sure this comes from tension and it will cause you to stab at the ball in a somewhat jerky fashion. You must encourage the putting stroke to remain smooth, which will not happen with a curtailed back stroke. Always feel that you are rolling the ball towards the hole, not hitting it at the hole.

The other fault of which the senior golfer is often guilty is moving his head at impact. This is particularly prevalent on the shorter putts where you are anxious to see if you have got the ball into the hole. We are not aware of it but we all seem to want to start turning our heads at impact. Particularly with the older person, as soon as the head starts to turn, so will the shoulders, which

will then affect the path on which the club head is swinging. I know it is a very difficult thing to make yourself do, especially when faced with a four footer for the match, but strike the ball and listen for it to drop in the hole. Keep your head perfectly still, watching the spot where the ball started. It is worth trying to discipline yourself into doing this. I will guarantee you will hear more putts drop than you will see drop!

As the years go by, your putting can, if you are not careful, get worse and worse. Undoubtedly, the main causes are anxiety and tension. This can be seen by looking at the careers of all the best Professionals who ever lived. There comes a time in all of their lives, sometimes sooner, sometimes later, but always inevitably, when, if you will excuse the modern vernacular, their 'bottle' goes. A short putt will be missed at a crucial stage;

Opposite: The longer the putt, the larger the pendulum so there is more momentum to propel the ball further. The pendulum is not a hitting movement; it takes care of strike and distance and has its own acceleration. Right: Keep the putter level with the ball's equator for at least nine inches on either side. Position the ball just inside the heel of the left foot.

This photographic sequence shows the pendulum putting swing from a different angle. The pendulum starts straight back from the ball and travels through impact to the throughswing, which should be equidistant to the backswing. Thus the blade should come through the ball the same distance as it went back.

Right: Your pendulum on the backswing may have been good but if you look up too soon to watch the ball drop into the hole, your head and body will turn and therefore the blade will turn to hit the ball to the left.

this may be followed by another the following week, maybe costing him the Tournament. Then the self-doubt starts creeping in. Those four footers start looking harder, the backswing starts getting a bit short, the grip starts to become a bit tighter and, before we know it, the decline of another great golfer is under way. He is still just as good from tee to green but, as usual, the putting is the first thing to fail.

Silly really isn't it, because after all is

Putting tip

If you are going through a particularly bad spell with your putting, try another putter. Because you are looking at a different head it often sharpens the concentration.

said and done 'all we have to do is hit the ball in the right direction at the right strength'?

Putting equipment

Liking the head design of your putter will boost your confidence when putting. The traditional flat blade putter is still popular but you can also buy heel and toe weighted putter heads with a wider sweet spot. Many Seniors find that these are more forgiving when hit off-centre and will hit putts

further. There are also mallet putters which have a thick club head from the face to the back. They are often heel and toe weighted internally. The head materials used for putters are many and varied, including brass, aluminium alloy, stainless steel, graphite and wood, to name but a few.

Far left: A traditional flat blade putter with a hickory shaft.
Left: A blade putter with a flange.

Above: Two variations on the heel and toe weighted putter; you can see the sighting lines on the left. These putters hit putts further on off-centre hits. Right: The wide triangular design of this putter gives you a long sighting line. Below: This putter has built-in weight adjustment parts which can be filled with solid metal or cork spaces.

Bunker shots

Firstly, remember that the Rules of Golf forbid you to ground your club at address or to allow the club head to make contact with the sand during the backswing.

Obviously, when faced with a bunker shot, you want to get as close to the hole as possible, but your first priority must be to extricate the ball at your first attempt.

When the ball lies in a greenside bunker there are several different shots you can employ, depending upon the type of bunker, the lie with which you are faced, and the texture of the sand. Let me explain the two most commonly needed.

The explosion shot

When faced with a lie on normal, reasonably loose soft sand, the explosion shot is the safest means of getting out of a bunker. The sand iron should be used and the club head should be encouraged to enter the sand about two inches before the ball, travel through the sand under the ball and emerge two to three inches after the ball.

You should use an exaggeratedly open stance for this shot, with your feet, hips and

shoulders all aiming to the left of the flag. However, the club face should remain square to the flag. You must stand with more weight on the left foot and attempt to leave it there throughout the swing; this will prevent any tendency to sway, a common fault with the older player, and also assist in reaching the

Right: Note that the weight is mainly favouring the left foot with the ball positioned opposite the inside of the foot. Opposite: The address position for the explosion shot with a sand iron. Hold the club head above the sand with an open stance, the blade pointing at the target.

bottom of the swing in the correct place. The ball should be positioned towards the left heel.

When making the swing, you must realise that as there will be a cushion of sand between the ball and the club face, you must make a longer, harder swing than for a pitch of the same distance played off the turf.

Therefore, you must use a fairly full swing, feeling that you are lifting the club by means of an early wrist cock on a steeper plane than for a normal shot and also allowing the club to swing along the same line as your feet and shoulders. This will encourage you to swing slightly across the intended line of the shot which, in turn, assuming the club face

Above: The wrists have hinged on the backswing. From the open stance the swing is taken back on the shoulder line, giving the impression of an out-to-in swing and a steep backswing. Right: From the full steep backswing the line of attack into the sand is steeper than normal.

Above left and above: The head has stayed in position with the weight fully on the left foot as the swing moves smoothly through to a full finish. The secret is not to make too short a backswing or there is a tendency to stab or jab at the ball, the club will dig too deeply into the sand and the ball will stay still and not move.

remains facing the flag, will assist the ball to climb quickly. This downswing should be initiated with a distinct dragging of the club by the left hand and arm which should pull the club head down, under the ball and through to a high finish. Special attention should be paid to using the back of the left hand to hold the club head square to the target line through the impact area.

At all costs this action should be kept smooth; the whole swing should be unhurried. A lot of senior golfers fall into the trap of making too short a backswing and, in

Bunker tip

If in doubt about achieving enough loft to lift the ball over a high front lip don't be frightened to play out sideways. In this game, discretion is often the better part of valour.

the resultant rush to hit the shot, stab or jab at the ball which, in turn, usually leads to digging the club too deep into the sand and leaving the ball in the bunker.

As the years go by, you will probably experience some difficulty in getting the ball up to the hole. If this is the case and you can genuinely say that you are entering the sand two inches before the ball and are following through properly, I suggest that you start to take less sand. By entering the sand one to one-and-a-half inches before the ball there will be less cushioning effect by the sand and greater distance can be achieved.

Bunker tip

If the ball is lying well on relatively firm sand and there is no steep lip to the bunker, often a putter can be used to very good effect.

Ball on hard packed or wet sand

For the explosion shot from soft sand we use a sand iron due to the fact that the back edge of the sole is proud of the front edge. This design feature helps the club head to ride

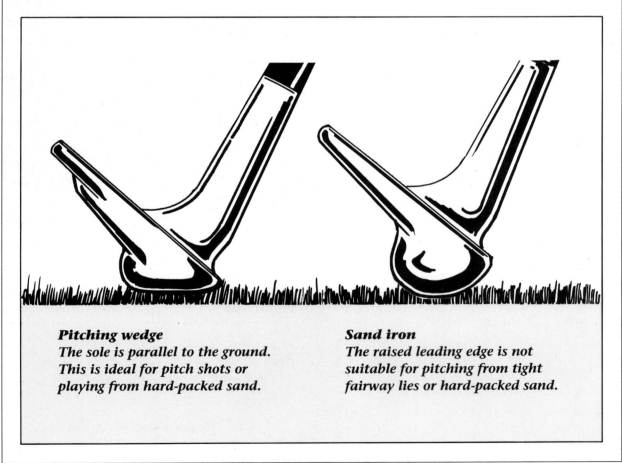

Pitching wedge
The sole is parallel to the ground. This is ideal for pitch shots or playing from hard-packed sand.

Sand iron
The raised leading edge is not suitable for pitching from tight fairway lies or hard-packed sand.

Above: Playing from hard-packed sand, use a pitching wedge and adopt a squarer stance than for an explosion shot. As usual, keep the weight on the left foot and then swing on a normal path.

back out of the sand rather than digging in too deep. However, if you attempt to use a sand iron on hard-packed sand, it will have a tendency to bounce off the surface and thin the ball.

Therefore you should use a pitching wedge for this shot as it will effectively cut

Above: The club is taken back less steeply on the backswing than for an explosion shot, and less sand is taken.

into this hard-packed surface and allow the club head to pass under and lift the ball.

For this shot, you should set up with a squarer stance but still keeping the weight on the left foot. You will swing now on a more normal path (flatter than for the explosion shot). The backswing need not be as long and the club head should enter the sand about an inch before the ball. As with the explosion shot, the swing should be kept smooth and unhurried. The downswing should still be made with a dominant left hand and arm pulling the club head down and through. These are the two shots that the senior golfer should practise and gain confidence in playing.

In this chapter, I have tried to explain the short game, albeit briefly. I have stuck to the few basic shots that you will keep coming across during your ventures on the golf course. Of course, there are variations and elaborations on all these shots, but to those of you who are just getting started in this great game of ours, simplicity should be the key word. If you are an established player who is beginning to see a decline in your endeavours, then I hope that I have refreshed the old memory and brought to your attention one or two thoughts that will help to stop the rot.

Common faults

By Les Jones

When playing or practising on the practice ground you will probably be hitting a lot of shots. Whatever department of the game you are working on you will hit the odd bad shot, be it wayward or just not feeling sweet off the club face. When you are playing a round of golf, the same thing happens unfortunately and I would put this down to just being human; you are not a machine, and all of us suffer from the bad shot here and there, even the best golfers amongst us. Being human, at times we lack concentration, chatting away to our partner and then playing the shot before we are ready. We can all be careless in the set-up position and thereby not settled in our minds on what the job at hand is about. Yes, we all have this little problem at times, and if it is not a persistent one, my advice is to realise what you have done and then forget it; all you have done for a shot or two is to have lost your pre-shot routine.

The danger otherwise is that you will look for faults in your swing and begin to try all kinds of remedies and minor adjustments to cure a problem that is not there. In doing so you will most certainly turn something that is very small into a major problem, a self-inflicted problem.

If your shots have a high percentage of mishits, then a fault has crept in that needs

Above: If you are too tense at address, the arms are too tight and the shoulders move upwards, making it difficult to move through 45 degrees. Opposite: You then fight to get the left shoulder round and the body moves up and away from the ball: this is not a controlled swing.

attention. To rectify this, you will need to know precisely what you are doing. Therefore, we will go through the basic faults that create the misbehaved shots. Firstly, a word of advice: if you have let yourself become mentally upset about your performance, please see your local

Above: This shows a bad movement down into the ball. Not started by a lateral hip movement, it has been initiated by the hands and wrists. The arms have become divided and the weight on the left side has moved outwards. The ball could finish anywhere right of target.

professional. He will point you in the right direction so that with practice you can sort yourself out.

Earlier we looked at the set up. We created a sequence of static positions and it is worth going through this sequence again, looking for points that have gone wrong and the possible consequences that lead to bad shot making. Many common faults emanate from a bad set-up. We will now go back to the basics and see how a faulty position can affect your swing. If you get it right, you should be able to avoid most common swing faults and problems.

The aim (blade)

You have set up with the bottom edge of the club head at right angles to the target. This is the correct position. Now if you turn the toe end of the blade slightly left, the blade becomes closed to the target line. If you swing the club correctly the blade will return to this closed position at impact. The ball will hook by the same token if the blade is aligned with the bottom leading edge pointing right of the ball-to-target line. If the blade is open, a slice can occur. So you must get this simple basic discipline right and aim correctly if you are to avoid these damaging faults.

The hold – slicing and hooking

The hold on the club must be in a neutral position as explained earlier in Chapter 1. In a weak grip, either one or both hands are too far left on the grip, i.e. the 'V's on either hand are pointing to the chin, or, worse, the left shoulder. When you swing, the hands will return to the neutral position, the blade will be open and the dreaded slice will be the devastating result.

Right: Although this is basically a good grip, the bottom finger of the right hand is not round the shaft. Consequently the grip will tend to slide up the 'V' towards the top of the backswing.

This hold position will cause the right shoulder to move out of position, the take-away will tend to move outside the ball-to-target line and the backswing will become too steep – a difficult position to recover from on the downswing.

If the hold on the club becomes too strong with either one or both hands too much to the right on the grip, with the 'V's

Above: Looking down the line, you can see how the shoulder alignment has become open. The problem here is that if you swing the club along the shoulder line, the resultant swing path will be out-to-in, or, in other words, a slice.

Above: A weak hold in which both hands are too much over to the left-hand side of the grip. This not only helps to create a slice but also pulls the right shoulder outwards, thereby giving an open shoulder position.

pointing more towards the right shoulder, the hands will return to neutral, the blade will be closed and a hook will be the result. This hold will also tend to lead the takeaway into a flat, too much on the inside line, and, again, it will be a struggle to recover on the downswing. You will see that it is not only a bad hold, but the chain reaction it sets off in these two instances is exactly the opposite of what you want to achieve. The fuse box to the problem is the hold, which creates the other faults, so you must follow the sequence and not say to yourself: "I am swinging out-to-in or in-to-out".

Left: A strong hold is when either or both of the hands are to the right-hand side of the grip. The pull of movement drops the right shoulder and pushes out the hips towards the target. The weight is on the left side instead of being distributed equally.
Above: The hold has pulled the shoulders out of alignment so that they are closed to the ball-to-target line. The tendency is to swing the club round the body very flat. The face will be closed at the top of the swing, and a hook is the best result that you can expect.

I cannot stress enough the importance of your set up and the problems it creates if it is incorrect. We have mentioned the hook and slice and the reason why these shots occur. They may be worrying but they are not difficult to identify and correct. It is possible to look more deeply into the causes, but most of them will not apply to you and the most common reason is an incorrect hold. Do not confuse your mind and muscles by trying every conceivable way to cure your bad shots; go for the fuse box and correct them from there. Common faults are what

Many senior players seem to favour a strong hold because it feels strong and therefore they mistakenly believe that they can hit the ball further. However, nothing could be further from the truth, and if you want to avoid these faults creeping into your game, you should stay with the correct hold.

the words suggest, and all golfers, even the best, go through these phases. Let us look at some more of these common faults.

Right: Here the left-hander has too strong a hold and this has created a problem. The stance and the hips are aimed in the right direction but the strong left-hand hold has pulled the shoulders into a closed position, which will create a hook.

Hitting the ground before the ball

On the long shots you may be standing too upright, or with the more senior players there may be a tendency to be too crouched. If you are too upright, the body will move downwards with the left side collapsing. Alternatively, if you are too crouched, the body will not clear in time and the movement will be too wristy. The result of both positions is the same – hitting the ground before the ball. The same applies in the short game, and is usually referred to as 'fluffing'. Here again, the over-crouch of the body will encourage a wristy action.

Apart from these points, look to your arms, which I consider to be the most important part of your set up. Remember that they create and maintain the radius of the swing. If your stomach is larger than it used to be, and this does tend to happen in your middle and later years, the arms may become parted or splayed as you address the ball, and they will almost certainly straighten up on the downswing. The fluffed shot is then on the cards; the bigger the splay, the more you will hit the ground before the ball.

Right: A good position has been spoilt because the arms have divided or splayed. The left arm is in a weaker position than the right, and the divided arms have had an effect on the club face, causing the blade to open. A quick cure is to feel that your forearms are kept comfortably close together. This tends to happen to more portly golfers with a middle-aged spread.

The over swing

For the senior golfer, this is not quite so pronounced as maybe in the younger players. Although you may have developed a good three-quarter swing movement, there are still small and what you might call over-cooked movements that may have crept into your swing which will make your good position at the top of the swing overdone – an over swing. Perhaps you have a weak grip, i.e. either one or both hands too far to the left of the grip. If so, the pressure can be too loose and you will then lose the co-ordination of wrists and arms. The wrists will work independently and this will take you

beyond the good position you usually have at the top of the swing.

If you have too much weight on your left side at set up, you will find the arms will divide or splay, as you move into the back-swing; the weight will not be transferred correctly and the arms will splay more as you progress into the backswing with the result that all control will be lost.

Right: The swing has been partly restricted by the weight being too much on the left side. Instead of the club being swung around the body, the arms have moved upwards and are badly divided. The hands and shaft are at a point over the head rather than in the ideal position between the head and right shoulder.

Above and right: Too much weight is on the left side, changing the angle of the legs. Note that the right leg is out of proportion to the top half of the body on the left side. The most natural backswing you could achieve from this position would be for the arms to move upwards as the weight increases on the left side and the shoulder turn becomes difficult.

Topping

This is the missed shot that sometimes plagues the senior player who is trying to achieve that extra little bit of length. It occurs when the tendency is to hold the club so tightly in the set up that the wrist action becomes unresponsive, with the result that you lose vital flexibility. As you get older and your muscles start to stiffen up a little, a flexible wrist action becomes more important than ever.

Left: The knees are very straight leading to an over-crouched position too far away from the ball. This position makes you depend on the top half of the body: the arms, hands and shoulders.

Knees too straight

By the same token, if the knees are too straight in the set up, a sideways rocking movement of the hips will be created instead of the natural turn that should occur automatically. This action is very unpredictable and makes it difficult to get to the bottom of the ball on the downswing.

Above and right: In trying to recover from the lack of movement in the legs, the body has begun its upward surge with the resultant upward movement of the head. This will inevitably produce a topped shot.

Practice drill

If topping is your problem, it is useful to practise short backward and forward swings. You should feel that the movement is a sweeping action with the club head brushing the turf. This is a good exercise for developing smooth control of the swing. If you do not play a lot of golf on a regular basis, you can spend just a few minutes a day practising this drill in your garden. It will certainly help you to keep in touch with your tempo and rhythm.

Head up

Moving the body downwards in the backswing gives you an upward surge of the body on the downswing and this, in turn, creates the so-called 'head up' phenomenon. Be careful as to how you interpret this; it is difficult for the head to come upwards on its own. However, you must not consciously try to keep the head down as this makes movement into and through the ball restricted and your swing will become jerky.

It might be a good idea to look at the ball for a little longer but do not keep your head down.

The shank

Of all the faults that can creep into your game, the shank is the most devastating problem of all. It can quickly become not only a physical fault but also a mental disease where you try almost every known remedy available to relieve yourself of this most awful shot. But where does it come from? How does it happen? And what can you do about it?

Firstly, you must look at your set up and go through the routine checks in the correct sequence as outlined earlier in the book. Concentrate on the five check points (static positions) and check that you are performing them correctly – rather than looking for things that may be wrong with your set up. Doing it this way, with the emphasis on getting it right, is a more helpful and positive approach that will only take a few minutes. However, the negative approach of seeking out factors that are wrong can only produce confusion and may

Above and right: This address position is good and does not suggest a shank. As you move through the ball, the club head is taking the correct path.

Above: The problem of the shank is now revealed. The arms and club head have not taken their natural swing path round the body. The arms have tried to steer the ball and have moved away out of position at impact. The ball will be hit on the neck of the club, causing a shank.

make matters worse. As already stated, a good set up eliminates a lot of swing faults.

So what causes the shank and how does it happen? The problem usually starts in the short game when you attempt to 'steer' the ball to the pin. Your backswing could be well executed in a good position but things go wrong during the downswing and then through impact. Instead of the arms remaining constant to the body, and the swing path direction being from in-to-square-to-in, the arms move away from the body on the downswing as you try to move them, together with the club head, towards the target. As the blade approaches the ball, it moves outside the ball-to-target line by about one inch. This brings your strike pattern from the centre of the face into the shank. If you understand the reason for the shank, the problem will disappear.

Summary

As a teacher of this wonderful game of golf, I practise regularly to maintain the standard of my own personal play. I also practise the faults that many golfers experience at some time in their life with their swing so that I can understand fully the reasons for hitting bad shots. In this way, I can demonstrate them to my class or pupils. I can almost produce any of those bad shots at will. I say 'almost' because, due to my practice, the good shots are still produced from my muscle memory, but with faulty actions that I impose on them for teaching purposes.

The shank is the most frightening swing fault of all, but if you understand the reason for its occurrence, you can cure it for ever. This advice goes for all the problem shots so if one of them is your problem, try and comprehend why it is happening and then go back to the set up and swing basics and focus on performing them correctly to cure your particular problem. Do not despair! All swing faults are curable, and you can create a swing that will work for you.

Trouble shots

By Les Jones

Ball under lip of bunker

I recently played nine holes with one of my more Senior members at the golf club – hence nine holes only! He hit the ball quite well for his age but on the 8th hole he was bunkered to the right of the green. The lie was one of those horrible positions three-quarters of the way up a steep slope. After struggling to take his stance, and trying to maintain some form of balance, he looked at me askance. "Have you considered," I asked, "playing sideways to safety? You then have the chance of a chip and putt on to the green which is a lot better than you can do by trying a shot from that position." It worked and although he chipped and two-putted, he was happy with the result. When you are facing a similar dilemma, remember the thinking game; play safe and work out your strategy.

Below: The ball is in such a difficult position that it is hard to get your balance and the swing could be restricted.

Right: As you try to accelerate the club head into the ball, you lose all control with arms and hands.

Above: The ground is hit before the ball and you are now losing balance totally. Above right: The result is that the ball rolls back into the bunker. Right: The correct way to deal with this shot is to accept a more balanced stance with a higher ball. All you need is a short shot of about 15 feet to get you to safety. A chip and a putt are on the cards but you have not wasted a shot and have been saved from trouble.

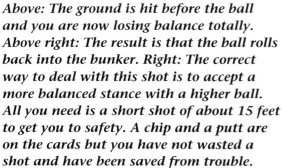

Long bunker shots

Long bunker shots are always a challenge so do not hurry them. Your train of thought must be: firstly, the lie of the ball in the sand. If it is tight or sitting down, you must get out to the nearest point of relief on the fairway, preferably the best spot to be in for your next shot. Secondly, if the lie is good, you must consider the height of the face of

the bunker you have to carry. This will affect your choice of club. If you think a 6 iron will take you to the green, use a 5 iron to swing the club easily and smoothly. The slightest tension will make you fluff the shot. Visualize the shot and the feel of the swing tempo. Set up as normal but position the ball more towards the left heel.

Left: Position the ball towards the left heel. Do not dig your feet into the sand, but stand on the edge, securely.

Shots over trees

When you are faced with a shot to the green with reasonably high trees in the way, you need a lofted club to get over them. Once this decision has been made, the trees are forgotten. Take up a slightly open stance with the ball positioned towards the left heel. This enables you to slide the blade under the ball, keeping the club face slightly open. The hold must not be tight; it should be quite relaxed because you need more flexibility to hit the ball higher.

Left and above: A liberal backswing is required and you must not try to consciously get the ball into the air. The ball position is forward in the stance.

Shots under trees

When you are hitting from under a tree or out of heather or gorse, which can restrict your backswing, your first priority is to get out but how far can you go without being greedy? This is an unnatural shot with an unnatural posture and stance. You will have to be very positive when playing it, but do not use too much physical effort. The most important thing to concentrate on is to keep the ball flying low.

Left: The hold is at the bottom of the grip to give more control. The ball is in the centre of the stance with the hands more forward than normal. The blade is slightly hooded.

Restricted swing

Above: The backswing is completely restricted and there is just as much a problem in front with the low branches of the trees. The hands are forward of the blade at address to create a steeper backswing. The delivery of the club into the *ball will feel more like a punch than a hit. The follow through will be at least as far as the backswing. Through the strike position, keep the hands ahead of the club head as they were positioned at address.*

Left: At address the hands are ahead. Below: The hands move into and through the ball and the club face stays square to slightly open. Even more importantly, the head and the body remain stable.

The positions are the same for playing a restricted swing as for the low shot, with the hands forward and the knees flexed. If you cannot stand your full height you will be hunched up with the hands lower down the shaft. Try one or two backswings to see how much room you have got to work within. You are bound to lose leverage and so you must accelerate into and through the ball via the hands and arms.

Ball above the feet

When the ball is above the feet, like in many awkward lies, an understanding of ball flight, stance and body position is of paramount importance. There is a tendency to hook the ball so allow for this by aiming slightly to the right of the target. The hold on the club should be slightly further down the grip than usual.

Left and above: Take up your normal address position with the weight more towards the toes. Swing mainly with your hands and arms. The ball will fly higher so take a club more than usual.

Ball below the feet

The ball below the feet is one of the most difficult lies of all. The flight of the ball will tend to slice, and the longer the shot, the bigger the bend on the ball. Therefore you should aim left of target. Because the ball is below you, it is important that you stay balanced throughout the shot. Hold the club at full length with the weight positioned more towards the heels.

Above left: Pull your stomach in to give yourself more bend from the waist. Flex your knees with the weight towards the heels. From this position you can maintain your balance and rhythm and swing with only the hands and arms.

Above: Although this slope is pronounced, because your posture has accommodated it, the slope does not look odd. The most important thing is not to fight it and create tension by trying to get a normal set up.

SENIOR GOLFER

Uphill and downhill lies

At set up with a downhill lie, the ball will tend to slice to the right, so aim left of target. Position the ball further back in the stance with the weight on the lower leg.

Bend the upper knee inwards to accommodate the slope, and swing the club with the hands and arms.

Left: When tackling a downhill lie, don't be greedy. Pick your spot as you may not get much distance with a steep slope. Work more on position and safety rather than on trying to propel the ball distances. On a normal lie, you would probably take a 5 iron, but on a steep slope like this you will need a 9 iron to get the ball airborne and forwards.

Reverse the procedure for uphill lies with the ball positioned more towards the left heel. It will tend to hook and fly higher so take a longer club to get the required distance. The hand and arm movement must stay smooth and rhythmical with little body movement or you will lose your balance.

Practice

By Tony Moore

t St Mellion, where I have the pleasure of being the Professional, we have a senior section. They arrange their own competitions and play matches against other golf clubs. To qualify to join the 'Fossils' as they call themselves, you have to be retired. This veterans section, as at most golf clubs, is a particularly active part of the club; time is now on their side. No longer the one round a week on a Sunday morning and rush home to lunch and an afternoon with the family.

A lot of senior golfers go to the club three or four days a week and play their round of golf no matter what the weather. I often see them teeing off on the first hole at 8 o'clock in the morning in conditions you wouldn't send a dog out in!

Because of the title of this book and the section of golfers at which it is aimed, I suspect that you might be one of these people, or at least will soon become one. With the amount of golf you play or soon intend to play, I wonder how often you practise?

Golf is a wonderful game and I always maintain that it does not matter how good or bad a golfer you are; you can still get a tremendous amount of fun out of the game. However, the better you become, the more enjoyment and satisfaction you are going to achieve.

For anyone to perform to the best of their ability they need to practise. Hopefully, by the time you have completed this book you will have gained some new ideas about various aspects of the game and be inspired to give them a try, but you are not suddenly going to master them whilst playing in your usual fourball. You must try to get to grips with any swing change on the practice ground. This is where you can start to gain the confidence to put that thought into practice on the golf course.

During my time at St Mellion, I have been privileged to see a veritable galaxy of golfing stars, both European and International, who have visited our course to compete in exhibition matches and the Benson & Hedges tournament. When I say stars I mean just that: Jack Nicklaus, Seve Ballesteros, Nick Faldo, Ian Woosnam, Tom Watson, Sandy Lyle, Bernhard Langer. The list goes on and on. On their arrival at the course the first question that they ask is: "Where is the practice ground?"

Club members often ask me why these world-class players need to practise. Surely when you are that good you don't need to practise? These players use the practice ground for one of three reasons: firstly to work on some aspect of their swing which they are trying to improve; secondly to simply keep their eye in and by continued practice maintain their swing and rhythm; and thirdly to hit golf balls to loosen up prior to a round of golf.

Quite frankly, to maintain, or

hopefully to improve, our game, we should all do the same. So I would like to look into these three areas of practice with particular regard to the senior golfer.

Practice guidelines

Let me give you one or two guidelines that I consider to be exceptionally important with regard to your time spent on the practice ground.

● Always warm up before any practice session. Spend two or three minutes practising swinging, starting with gentle half swings and gradually building the rhythm,

tempo and length of the swing to that which you are about to use on the shots you are going to play. In short, loosen those muscles and joints, giving them prior warning of what is to come.

● The average 18 handicap golfer will probably hit a maximum of 40 full shots during the course of a round of golf. Therefore do not expect your body to be able to sustain a practice session where a vast number of shots are attempted. I would suggest that 40 balls struck over a period of

Below: Do not practise too often in the nets as it can create little faults.

30 to 40 minutes is ideal. The object is not to exhaust yourself. Take your time between shots: it should not become a race to hit as many balls as possible as quickly as you can. To this end I would suggest that you place your practice bag 10 yards away from where you are hitting and make yourself walk to collect the next ball.

I suggest 30 to 40 minutes, not only to encourage you not to rush these 40 shots, but also because you will find it difficult to maintain maximum concentration much beyond this point.

● Always lay a club on the ground outside the ball, taking time to check that it is parallel to the target line. With the assistance of this aid, constantly check your club face

alignment, ball position and stance. Although this second club will not be with you on the course you will soon get used to standing correctly without its aid.

● Do not let a practice session become a slogging session. Concentrate mainly on hitting shots with a 6 or 7 iron. If you normally expect to hit your 6 iron, say, 30 yards, position yourself that distance from a given target. You should then attempt to hit that target, not to hit that 6 iron as far as you possibly can or to hit it aimlessly into an open field.

● If the wind is blowing and you have a tendency to slice, do not practise hitting balls through a left-to-right wind (the opposite applies if you hook). This will only exaggerate any tendency you have to bend the ball and will certainly mean that the session does you more harm than good. If the wind is blowing really hard forget practice altogether and retire to the

Above: The ball is positioned inside the ball-to-target line and outside the stance line. Practise hitting the ball with these two guidelines to help you.

clubhouse! A strong wind makes the production of good shots very difficult as it encourages us to brace ourselves against its force, to grip too tightly and to swing too fast. The whole idea of practice is to help us to improve and thereby build our confidence; this does not happen in a strong wind so do not bother trying.

Improving your swing

During these pages I hope we have given you several new thoughts or perhaps jogged your memory with several old thoughts as to how to tackle the various shots with which you are confronted during a round of golf. However, the golf course is not the place to experiment with newly discovered ideas. Take them to the practice ground and attempt to put them into effect there. Give this new idea that you are interested in utilizing a chance. Loosen up thoroughly before you begin. With the help of the club on the ground make sure that everything (club head, grip, stance alignment, posture etc.) is in order before you swing. Concentrate on the new thought, firstly with practice swings. When you feel ready, try out the idea with the ball but do not expect immediate success. All alterations to the swing take a while to show consistent results – ask Nick Faldo.

I am approached frequently by newly retired people who say that they have often fancied taking up golf but now they have the time, are they too old? Of course the answer is that they will almost certainly never be scratch players but equally they are certainly not too old to start and with patience and application reach a reasonable standard.

I feel that I can teach a twelve-year-old to swing the club well and produce some really acceptable shots within a few weeks of first handling a golf club. Unfortunately, the older player inevitably takes longer to acquire these new movements that comprise the golf swing and so must dedicate a certain amount of time on the practice ground between lessons to develop his or her new-found skills. This person, the beginner or relative novice to the game, must be especially careful and disciplined in his or her practice sessions. It can be all too easy to 'give in' on a particular swing thought and revert to doing what comes naturally and is a more comfortable movement or position. The whole purpose of practice is to master a particular aspect of the game – not to instill an incorrect movement.

General practice

Even when you feel at peace with your game and feel that you are striking the ball well, I would still encourage regular practice sessions. There is nothing more satisfying than hitting a succession of really well struck shots one after the other. It builds your confidence and keeps you in the mood for a good round next time you play.

Beware the practice session when you are hitting the ball really well! There will be a great tendency to try to hit the ball further. Although you may get away with this to a degree, sooner or later the shots will deteriorate due to a loss of rhythm. Make

sure you hit to a target that is positioned at the range of the club you are using. Try to realise why the shots are going so well. Invariably it will be due to a relaxed rhythmic swing. Encourage this; encourage your body to turn and unturn; encourage a wide sweeping arc by swinging the arms back and through. Try to feel the weight of the club head as it swishes through the ball.

Warm up first

How often do you arrive at the golf club, put on your golf shoes and proceed to the first tee fully expecting to play well? The majority

of golfers do this and usually, when asked how they played, say they played quite well apart from the first few holes.

Get into the habit of leaving home 20 minutes earlier than normal to give yourself the time to 'warm up' prior to playing. Spend a couple of minutes practice swinging, then hit several short pitch shots, increase the length of the swing to hit fuller shots, then progress to a few 7 irons, all the time keeping the swing smooth and easy. Finish your warm up with one or two chip shots and five minutes of putting, concentrating on the two to five footers. By going through this routine you are giving yourself an excellent chance of getting your round off to a flying start and hopefully taking the money off the opposition!

As we get older it should be realised that this pre-game practice routine gets more necessary. It allows us to build up that all-important rhythm of the swing before stepping on to the first tee. I always feel that if you do not take it to the first tee you won't find it while out on the course.

Below: It is a good idea to finish your warm up with this drill. Set up a line of balls and then practise putting them in sequence towards the hole. This will help you to improve your putting stroke and achieve more consistency – very valuable commodities on the green.

Exercises

As the years go by it is even more important that we look after our bodies. We become more susceptible to muscular strains and injuries and, probably more to the point, they take longer to heal. Prior to play or practice, make it a golden rule to go through a routine of warm-up loosening exercises. Here is one for you to try.

1 Stand erect and, with hands on hips, rotate to the right and then to the left. This should be done in a slow relaxed manner, not straining to turn your shoulders too far to start with. This movement should be repeated until the upper body can comfortably turn through 90 degrees to the right, then 90 degrees to the left.

2 Now, keeping your legs straight, lean forwards from the waist as though attempting to touch your toes. Again, this should be done slowly and gently and repeated several times. Don't worry – I do not expect you to actually touch your toes! However, this exercise will just start to stretch the muscles in the lower back.

3 Place a golf club behind and across your back holding it in position in the crook of your elbows. Now adopt your normal address posture, i.e. flexed knees, leaning forwards from the waist, and while running the club against your back, turn to the right as if making a backswing, then turn to the left as though making a follow through.

Do not overdo any of these exercises – all these movements should be slow and relaxed. Never be too vigorous or try to turn or stretch further than you can and feels comfortable. However, as your muscles loosen and these exercises take effect, you will find that you will be capable of turning further and further.

This exercise is for keeping the body flexible and loose. Holding the club in front of you make a normal swing. Keep the left arm firm and the body stable. The right arm maintains the radius of the movement through. If no club is available, you can perform this exercise with a rolled-up towel. Do it as part of your warm-up routine before you play, and for a few minutes each day to keep your golf muscles supple.

Tuition

You are obviously interested in improving your golf or you would not be reading this now. I sincerely hope that you will have gleaned a lot of useful advice and ideas. Even so I cannot stress too strongly the need for individual tuition from a PGA Professional. Before I hear you say that you are too old for that sort of thing, let me assure you that you are not! This applies particularly to those of you who are relatively new to golf, but also to the established player. The experienced professional will help the newcomer to the game to master the basis of grip, stance and swing that will then give him or her an excellent chance of success at the game.

With the established player, he will point out one or two aspects of the individual's game which are letting him or her down. Don't worry – he will not try to change your swing completely, but will probably ask you to make one or two minor alterations. Remember that he makes his living teaching the game of golf. He wants you to improve. He does not want the bad publicity you will give him if your game deteriorates.

During a lesson, do not be afraid to ask questions. Stop him if you do not understand what he is talking about. If he suggests you alter your grip or narrow your stance, ask him why. Once you have the logical reasoning that supports a change, you are more likely to persevere with and master that alteration.

If you are just starting out in golf, a course of half a dozen or so lessons, taken once a week, is essential. For the more established golfer a regular check up every three to four months is highly recommended. Your golf professional is there to help you, so make use of him.

Positive Practice

Many golfers I know, both young and old, tell me that they rarely, if ever, visit the practice ground because they find practising boring. I wonder if you are one of those people? I have already offered quite a few constructive, practical hints on how to go about tackling a practice session. So now let me take it one step further – let us think about the mental side of practice.

Do not go to the practice ground by yourself. Take Jack Nicklaus along with you! Or take Lee, Arnie, Seve or whoever is your golfing hero. In your mind they will always hit the target green with their iron shots. You must try to match them. They will always get down in two with their chip and pitch shots. You must try to match them. They will never 3 putt and always hole from inside five feet. Again you must match them.

You may think this idea a little childish. Maybe it is, but it will certainly sharpen up your mind and get you to really try on each shot you hit. Get involved in your own fantasy and imagine the crowds around the green. Listen to the applause for the good shot, or alternatively hear the groans after a bad one.

This idea will spice up any practice session and if you are imaginative enough should certainly eliminate the boredom. However, this theme that I call 'positive practice' does have a more positive purpose

than simply making your practice session more entertaining. I wonder if you are one of the multitude of golfers, both low and high handicappers, who can go to the practice ground and hit virtually every shot perfectly acceptably, but during the course of a competitive round of golf the good shots are very few and far between and some of the bad ones don't even bear thinking about.

The reason for this Jekyll and Hyde difference between practice ground and course is probably two-fold. On the practice ground you are standing in the same place, hitting from the same lie, using the same club and hitting shot after shot. You will soon get into a consistent rhythm and will produce a lot of good shots. On the course things are different. Each shot is played with a different club from a different lie and with an appreciable time gap while walking between shots.

The other thing, and the main reason why I suggest our fantasy practice session with Jack, is that when hitting shots one after the other on the practice ground there is no pressure. Not only do you get into a relaxed rhythm but also it does not matter if you hit a bad shot. Hitting the good shot on the golf course is a totally different matter. You only have the one chance. You must hit the fairway, you must carry that cunningly placed bunker or you must avoid the pond or

you must hole that putt.

Therefore, when practising you must try to put yourself under the same type of pressure. This 'positive practice' in your fantasy world is one of the best practice ideas that I can give you.

Just imagine that you and Arnold Palmer are playing together, leading the field through the final round of the Seniors Championship! The pressures you are then

Above: Make time to practise the shots you may encounter out on the golf course. Be positive in your practice sessions without putting yourself under pressure. You will then be better prepared to get out of trouble if you meet it during a game.

faced with during your club's monthly medal will pale into insignificance.

Conclusion

One of the most memorable occasions that I ever witnessed happened during the 1973 Open Championship at Troon when Gene Sarazen holed in one at the Postage Stamp hole. He was 71 years old!

James Braid, one of the first great champions of the game of golf, had the distinction of playing Walton Heath every year from the age of 68 to a score equal to or below his age.

A certain Mr Bernard Matthews carded a gross 70 at his local course, Banstead Down Golf Club, in 1988 at the grand old age of 82.

I mention these random facts to illustrate that as old age creeps up on us, all is not lost. Modifications to the swing and stance may be necessary, a few yards may be lost and your handicap may creep up the odd slot. Nevertheless keep on practising. I bet those three gentlemen did.

Index

Numbers in *italics* refer to illustrations.

A

Aim, 10, 119
Alignment, 17
Arm movement, 40

B

Backswing, 11, 13, 31, 37, 41, 42, 137
  for pitch shot, 92
Ball above feet, 139
Ball below feet, 140
Ball position, 18
  in shots over trees, 135
  in shots under trees, 136
Ball-to-target line, 10, 17
Baseball grip, 16, *16*
Braid, James, 158
Bunker shots, 76, 108-114
  explosion shots, 108-112
  long, 134
Bunkers, 108-114
  ball under lip of, 132-133

C

Chip shot, 77-78
  executing, 84-89
Chipper stroke, 80-81
Clubs, 8
  grips, 54-56
  head design, 52-53
  ladies', 55
  lie of, 49
  senior, 54
  shafts, 53
  utility, 53
  weight of, 53
Course management, 57

D

Distance from ball, 19-20
Distances, 58

Divots, 49,50
Downhill lies, 141
Downswing, *30-31*, 123
Drivers, 18
  metal-headed, 53
  wooden heads, 53
Driving, 48, 59-62

E

Equipment, 8, 49-56
  long game, 49
  putting, 106-107
Exercises, 151-154
Explosion shots, 108-112

F

Fairway woods, 62-64
Flexibility, 41,135
Follow through, 34-35

G

Grip(s), 11-16, 119
  baseball, 16, *16*
  cack-handed, 98, *98*
  interlocking, 15, *15*
  jumbo, 55
  left-hand, 11, *11*
  left-handed, 16, *16*
  overlapping, 14, *14*
  putting, 97-99
  reverse overlap, 98, *98*
  right hand, 12-14, *12-14*
  strong, 121
  weak, 119-120
  Vardon, 14, *14*

H

Head design, 52-53
Hooking, 119, 121, 122

I

Impact, 34
Interlocking grip, 15, *15*
Irons, 52
  long, 65-69

sand, 90, 112

J

Jumbo grips, 55, *56*

L

Ladies' clubs, 55
Left-handed grip, 16, *16*
Lies, 62
  downhill, 141
  grassy, 66
  tight, 67
  uphill, 142
Long game, 47-72
  equipment, 49
Long irons, 65-69

M

Mind game, 45-46

N

Nicklaus, Jack, 49

O

One-piece takeaway, 28-29, *28-29*
Overlapping grip, 14, *14*
Over swing, 124, *125*

P

Par 4's, 70-72
Pendulum swing, 86, 103, *103, 104-105*
Persimmon heads, 53
Physical build, 41-42
Pitch shot, 78-79, 90-95
Pitching clubs, 18
Player, Gary, 69
Posture, 19-21
  in putting, 99-100
Practice, 9, 36, 143-158
  for backswing, 31
  guidelines, 145-148
  for short game, 76
Putters, 106-107

Putting, 96-107
    equipment, 106-107
    grips, 97-98
    posture, 99-100
    stroke, 100-106

R

Reading greens, 96-97
Relaxation, 9, 24
Restricted swing, 41, 43, 132, 137
Rhythm, 31, 35
Running shot, 77

S

St Mellion Golf Club, 57, 60-62, 70-72, 74
Sand irons, 90, 112
Sarazen, Gene, 158
Set up, 7-24
    building a routine, 22-23, *22-23*
    for woods, *63*
Shafts, 54
Shank, 128-130
Short game, 73-114
Slicing, 119, 121
Snead, Sam, 65
Stance, 17, 22, 23

for chip shot, 84
for pitch shot, 91
too wide, 41, *41*
Static positions, in set up, 10-21
Sweet spot, 53
Swing, 25-46
    backswing, 31, 37
    downswing, 30-31, *30-31*
    follow through, 35
    impact, 34
    improving, 148
    one-piece takeaway, 28-29, *28-29*
    restricted, 41, 43, 132
    weight transference, 28
    wrist action in, 39, *39*, 40
Swing faults, 115-130
    hitting ground before ball, 123, *133*
    hooking, 119, 121, 122
    over swing, 124, *125*
    shank, 128-130
    slicing, 119, 121
    tense at address, 116-119
    topping, 126-127

T

Texas wedge, 82-83

Topping, 126-127
Trees, 135-138
    shots over, 135
    shots under, 136
Tuition, 155

U

Uphill lies, 142

V

Vardon grip, 14, *14*
Visualization, 89

W

Waggle, 26,*26*, 27
Warm up, 149-150, *151-154*
Wedges, 86, 90, 112
Weight transference, 28
Women golfers, 21, *21*
Woods, 53, 59
    fairway, 62-64
    versus irons, 67
Wrist cock, 32, 33, 35, 39, 40, 69
    in bunker shots, 110

Y

Yardage charts, 58, *58*

Acknowledgements

The publishers would like to thank the following for their kind assistance in the creation of this book.

Arwyn Davies

Ben Hogan Ltd

Captain L.A. Harpum R.N. Secretary of Woodbridge Golf Club

Anne Seward, a member of Woodbridge Golf Club

St Mellion Golf Club